Acclaim for Catholic Baby Names
for Girls and Boys

"**What's in a name?** As one who always signs her middle initial in honor of our Blessed Mother's *fiat*, I can testify to the potential for evangelization every time I discuss my name. With *Catholic Baby Names for Girls and Boys: 250 Ways to Honor Mary*, Katherine Morna Towne encourages us to think outside the box when selecting names. I was delighted to learn of the many variations, including valiant tributes to Our Lady for boys. A perfect gift or family resource!"

— Lisa M. Hendey, Founder of CatholicMom.com
and author of *The Grace of Yes*

"*Catholic Baby Names* for Girls and Boys: 250 Ways to Honor Mary is the Catholic baby name aficionado's dream come true. Presenting hundreds of Marian names, Towne has masterfully organized and meticulously researched name meanings and origins so you can spend delightful hours perusing names, familiar and unfamiliar alike. A must for expecting Catholic moms and dads!"

— Haley Stewart, writer, speaker, podcaster and the
voice behind the blog, *Carrots for Michaelmas.*

"**Joyful, fascinating,** and rigorously researched, this book is a delight to read, whether you're getting ready for a baby or just love names."

— Simcha Fisher, writer, speaker, and author of
The Sinner's Guide to Natural Family Planning

"*Catholic Baby Names* for Girls and Boys: 250 Ways to Honor Mary is amazing. I can picture every expectant Catholic couple cuddled together reading this book thinking of names for their unborn babe. I didn't realize how many names there were for Mary, and some

are so unique, but I feel those kind of names (with more traditional nicknames) are all the rage!"

— Colleen Martin, blogger at *Martin Family Moments*

"Everyone knows that Mary is the tops when it comes to Catholic baby names, but you can't possibly name your whole big Catholic family after Our Lady! Or can you? This gem of a resource by Katherine Morna Towne gives an unbelievable wealth of names to honor the Blessed Mother, including those that are a bit obscure, cool, and absolutely beautiful!"

— Tommy Tighe, author of *The Catholic Hipster Handbook.*

"Choosing a name for your child is not to be taken lightly and as Catholics, we are encouraged to choose a name that will somehow reflect the gift of faith we will bestow upon our babies at Baptism and for the rest of their lives. So what's a Catholic parent to do? Enter *Catholic Baby Names for Girls and Boys: 250 Ways to Honor Mary.* This book provides a beautiful, meaningful collection of Marian names for both girls and boys. Its easy-to-read format includes an alphabetical list of names along with their meanings and origins. Other interesting tidbits about the Marian monikers and our Catholic faith are marbled in throughout this treasury. This book is sure to be a wonderful helpmate for expectant parents and would make a lovely baby shower gift. And what better way to honor Our Blessed Mother than to gift a child with a Marian name!"

— Kate Wicker, speaker, and author of *Getting Past Perfect: Finding Joy and Grace in the Messiness of Motherhood* and *Weightless: Making Peace with Your Body.*

"In today's culture, parents-to-be desire to give their children distinct names that set the tone for who they will become in life. Catholic parents everywhere are following this trend, and no one is better equipped than Katherine Towne to help parents select names that suit their taste, while also invoking some powerful patrons. Kate has

done this for years via her blog, Sancta Nomina, and now parents everywhere can own this beautiful resource to honor the Blessed Mother by name in various ways. This extensive list is sure to help those seeking to honor Our Lady select a name that fits their unique tastes and naming requirements, while teaching them a thing or two about Mary's impact on the world throughout Church history. I loved Kate's commentary throughout, and cannot recommend this resource highly enough for those looking to honor Our Lady in the naming of their child."

— Heather McQuillan, co-host of "Go Forth with Heather & Becky" podcast

"This book is a treasure trove of Marian names, from Achiropita to Zinnia for girls and from Alan to William for boys. While reading, I was thrilled to discover Marian connections to some of my kids' names that I'd never realized before! *Catholic Baby Names for Girls and Boys: 250 Ways to Honor Mary* is a must-have for any Catholic parent's bookshelf, especially for those who, like me, are obsessed with baby names and their meanings."

— JoAnna Wahlund, "The Catholic Working Mother," www.catholicworkingmother.com

"What an honor it is for parents to name their children! And what a precious opportunity to call upon saints who have gone before us and to ask their intercession for our children. There can be no saint more worthy of honor than Our Lady herself, and this book helps us to ask her intercession in creative ways, by sharing hundreds of names with which to do it. In these pages, we all benefit from the painstaking and thorough research Katherine Morna Towne has lovingly accomplished. Such a fascinating history of Our Lady and compilation of her feast days and special honors! Whether you are an expectant parent looking for a unique way to honor the Blessed Virgin Mary, or simply

a "name junkie" like so many of us, you will love perusing these pages and will come away inspired!"

— **Danielle Bean,** writer, speaker, brand manager at Catholic Mom.com and co-host of "The Gist" on CatholicTV

"Choosing a Marian name for your baby, or helping your teen select a Confirmation name, just got easier. Kate Towne takes the guesswork out of the naming process, offering hundreds of names and nicknames that refer to Mary or are used in her honor. Complete with feast-day information, a bit of history, and plenty of variations and cross-referencing, this guide to names that honor the Blessed Mother is fascinating and full of surprises."

— **Barb Szyszkiewicz,** OFS, writer and editor at CatholicMom.com

"As an avid blog reader and baby name enthusiast I was ecstatic when I heard Kate wrote a book. I had high hopes for *Catholic Baby Names for Girls and Boys: 250 Ways to Honor Mary* and my expectations were far exceeded. Kate is an expert at explaining the significance behind the name but also providing thoughtful and unique nicknames for virtually any name. This book is a must-have for all Catholic families. I would've loved to peruse this as a child!"

— **Grace Patton,** blogger at *Camp Patton*

"Kate Towne has given Catholic parents — and the entire Church — a beautiful treasure in her book of Marian names for boys and girls. Drawing from a rich tradition of honoring the holy name of Mary and incorporating many of her apparitions and titles of honor, Towne delves deep into the history and riches of Catholicism and emerges with some real treasures. From the ordinary to the more extraordinary, this book is an invaluable resource for expectant parents and a worthwhile addition to any parish library."

— **Jenny Uebbing,** *Mama Needs Coffee* blog

"With this meticulously researched book, Kate offers Catholic families many paths to choosing a name honoring Our Lady. From the most traditional to the truly offbeat, her thoughtful suggestions for Marian names prove that it's possible to combine spiritual meaning and modern style. If you're looking for twenty-first century names deeply rooted in millennia of Catholic faith, start with this resource to find the exactly right name for your child."

— *Abby Sandel,* founder of Appellation Mountain and columnist at Nameberry

"One might think that the subject of Marian names — those related to the Virgin Mary — might be a rather limited one, but Katherine Morna Towne has given ample proof that it is not in her fascinating new book on the subject. Including male names as well as female, this product of a decade of impeccable research includes titles, events and places related to Mary herself, some intriguing, wide-ranging trivia with cultural references ranging from the botanical to Sleeping Beauty to TV sitcoms, and with Towne's genuine subjective views adding into the mix. Recommended not only to those with a Catholic perspective but all name nerds as well."

— Linda Rosenkrantz, co-founder of Nameberry.com and co-author of ten books on names

"This book is a must-read for any expectant mother wanting to honor Mary in naming her child. If this book had been around eight years ago, my daughter Isabel would surely have Edelweiss as a middle name! Inspiring and well-researched, a perfect addition to the bookshelf of every growing Catholic family!"

— Rachel Balducci, writer, newspaper columnist, author of, and co-host of "The Gist" on CatholicTV

"Catholic Baby Names *for Girls and Boys: 250 Ways to Honor Mary* is a must-have for every Catholic home! As a fellow "name person," I pored over the richly described, Catholic names that are held within, complete with history, nicknames, pronunciations, feast days and

so much more! Kate has poured so much love and research into this book; bringing with it a true devotion to Our Lady and the communion of saints. This is truly a book that will be cherished for generations to come."

— *Sharon Clark*, Sole Proprietor of Baby My Love

"This unique book showcases the beauty and reverence embodied by Marian names. Thanks to the depth of historical information that Ms. Towne provides, the individuality of each homage shines through. And on a practical note, her attention to nicknames shows how versatile these names can be in appealing to parents' sense of style as well."

— Laura Wattenberg, creator of BabyNameWizard.com
and author of *The Baby Name Wizard*

"Kate's book came at the perfect time. My husband and I were stumped for Marian names for our 4th daughter! We wanted one that fit our family's style, was overt enough that it was obviously given in Our Lady's honor, and yet one that was also unique. Our daughter's name was found in the pages of this book, and I'm so grateful for it.

We found the book to be well-organized, easy to read and enjoyable as well! I even learned a number of interesting facts about the Blessed Mother's approved apparitions and some of her most dedicated saints. In a time when Catholic parents are searching for both creative and traditional names, this book offers many suggestions in a variety of styles. Hopefully this book will serve also to bring many more children under the mantle of Mary's protection."

— *Micaela Darr*, writer and birth educator at MicaelaDarr.com

"What's in a name? A lot more than I for one ever imagined. Katherine Morna Towne's loving and witty, story- and history-packed paean to Marian inspired names might have been subtitled "Towards a Theology of Onomatology." Names can be almost sacramental. What

their origins, variations and meanings might suggest reveals the fathomless mystery of the persons who will bear them and, if gifted with a Marian name, the special person they honor. This book is a godsend for anyone naming loved ones, rooting their identities for life in the Mother who gave the world the Name that gives life."

— *Bishop Edward Scharfenberger,* bishop of the Roman Catholic
Diocese of Albany, NY

For my Mom and Dad,
who have encouraged me with enthusiasm,
confidence, and prayer my whole life and through every step
of writing this book

and

for my husband and our six boys,
who have been patient with and excited for me throughout
this process, and without whose cooperation this book
could not have come to fruition.

Catholic Baby Names for Girls and Boys

Over 250 ways to honor Our Lady

By Katherine Morna Towne

Available from;
Marian Helpers Center
Stockbridge, MA 01263

Orderline: 1-800-462-7426
Websites:marian.org
ShopMercy.org

Publication Date:
2018

Imprimi Potest:
Very Rev. Kazimierz Chwalek, MIC
Provincial Superior
The Blessed Virgin Mary, Mother of Mercy Province
November 22, 2017

Nihil Obstat:
Dr. Robert Stackpole, STD
Censor Deputatus
November 22, 2017

Library of Congress Catalog Number: 2018938045
ISBN: 9781596144279

Designed by Catherine M. Shirley

Table of Contents

Introduction

People who love names *love* names. I have always been one of those people. Since the time I was a teenager, I've collected books of baby names of all different themes, and made lists (and lists!) of the names my future children would have. On all my girl lists, I always tried to have a form of Mary for either the first or middle name, just like my parents — and many Catholic parents — did with their daughters. And though I love the familiar Marian names (Mary, Marie, Maria, etc.), I was always intrigued when I happened upon a Marian name that I'd never considered or encountered. But it wasn't until I met a little girl whose middle name was *Immaculata* — a name I'd never heard for someone whom I knew — that I fell in love with the idea of researching and compiling all the Marian names I could find, so that other Catholic parents would have a resource for finding the perfect tribute to Our Lady.

I started with my baby name books and favorite baby name websites, then branched out to general Internet searches, scouring discussion boards and reader comments on name sites, searching for all names that referred to Mary or had been bestowed in her honor, and I added in names that I thought could be feasible as first, middle, and/or Confirmation names, even if they'd rarely, if ever, been used as given names. I then researched each name, in order to incorporate all my favorite aspects of other name books: pronunciation, history and other commentary, nicknames, and variants as well as examples from real life, literature, and/or culture. I was particularly pleased when I realized how many *male* names could be considered to be Marian, and also how many male saints, priests, brothers, and laypeople have a form of Mary in their names.

An immense blessing came in the form of my blog *Sancta Nomina*: Thoughts on Catholic baby naming (SanctaNomina.net) — an effort that started as a place for me to compile all the name resources important to me as a Catholic parent and "namiac" (as my mom calls

me!). *Sancta Nomina* has turned into a beautiful community for those who love the names of our faith, and I've gotten many new ideas for this book from my readers.

A few technical details: When writing the pronunciations, I relied heavily on Merriam-Webster's *Guide to Pronunciation,* as well as the pronunciations shared at Behind the Name and on the online audio pronunciation site Forvo (and others, to a lesser extent).[1] I tried to offer the pronunciations most Americans might encounter, and I apologize for any mistakes or misunderstandings on my part regarding subtleties of pronunciation, especially when it comes to other languages. When there were several variants of a name, I made subjective judgments about which should be the lead name in the entry (e.g., Annabel instead of Amabel, even though Annabel is said to have arisen from Amabel), and some variants received their own entries because I wanted to call attention to them. When I listed variants, I also listed the main language(s) in which they're used, if relevant, with an eye to brevity (i.e., one main language as much as possible, and "various" used when the name truly appears in several languages); and I don't claim to have included every possible variant of every name. Nicknames are a mix of traditional nicknames for each name and my own ideas of what's possible. Basically, I saw this effort as an intersection of scholarship, tradition, and real-life usage, and if there are any errors in any of those areas, please know that my intentions were pure.

Regarding the flower and plant names herein, though I only included certain ones, I want to point out that Vincenzina Krymow, in her book *Mary's Flowers: Gardens, Legends & Meditations*, asserts, "It is thought that at one time all flowers and plants honored Mary, the 'Flower of Flowers,' in legend or in name."[2]

Finally, a note about Baptismal and Confirmation naming requirements: In the old days the rules were quite strict about the names that could be bestowed upon a child at baptism — Woodeene Koenig-Bricker writes in her book *A Saint's Name: A comprehensive listing of Christian and Biblical names*, that under the *Code of Canon Law* in place from 1917 until 1983, "parents were **required** to give

their children a 'Christian' name. If they did not do so, then the pastor was obligated to add a saint's name."[3] *The Code of Canon Law* changed in 1983, and the new naming requirements are not so strict: Canon 855 states that "Parents, sponsors, and the pastor are to take care that a name foreign to Christian sensibility is not given." Basically, most names are fine, though the *Catechism of the Catholic Church* still shows a preference for legitimately Christian names, stating, "In Baptism, the Lord's name sanctifies man, and the Christian receives his name in the Church. This can be the name of a saint, that is, of a disciple who has lived a life of exemplary fidelity to the Lord. The patron saint provides a model of charity; we are assured of his intercession. The 'baptismal name' can also express a Christian mystery or Christian virtue" (CCC, 2156).

There aren't any specified guidelines for choosing a Confirmation name in the *Code of Canon Law* nor in the *Catechism*, so it seems wise to apply the same guidelines used for Baptism. Therefore, any of the names listed in this volume should qualify as appropriate choices for Confirmation (subject to the discretion of the local pastor).

People often name their children after those they consider to be worthy of respect, imitation, and honor, whether they be saints or celebrities, Biblical characters or political figures. I hope that when choosing a name — whether your child's given name or your own Confirmation or religious name — this volume inspires you to consider a name that honors the only person God handpicked to be the mother of His Son. For in so honoring her, you honor Him.

Feast of the Most Holy Name of Mary:
September 12

This volume seeks to offer as many ways to honor Our Lady as there are different tastes in names. The reason for naming our children after the Mother of God is well explained by St. John Chrysostom, who wrote, "So let the name of the saints enter our homes through the naming of our children, to train not only the child but the father, when he reflects that he is the father of John or Elijah or James; for, if the name be given with forethought to pay honor to those that have departed, and we grasp at our kinship with the righteous rather than with our forebears, this too will greatly help us and our children. Do not because it is a small thing regard it as small; its purpose is to succour us."[4]

Thus, choosing names that honor Mary will allow love for and devotion to her to enter our homes and families and remain in our minds and hearts.

But despite the many interesting, unusual, and creative ways to name someone after Our Lady, the name Mary itself is special. Though it has different forms in different languages, her name is called "Most Holy" by the Church, who has even instituted a feast day specifically in honor of it: September 12.

The Feast of the Most Holy Name of Mary was set for the universal Church after one of the many occasions in which Our Lady's powerful intercession was given. Though the feast originated in Spain, having been approved as a local celebration in 1513, it wasn't extended to the universal Church until 1683, when Christian Europe was saved from a Turkish Muslim army through Our Lady's intercession. As Fr. Donald Calloway, MIC, relates in his book *Champions of the Rosary:*

> In the 17th century, the Ottoman Turks (Muslims) were once
> again on a rampage in Eastern Europe, besieging town after

town in their efforts to spread Islam. In 1683, they made their way toward the key city of Vienna. They had tried to take the city before and failed, but now, with an army of more than 150,000 soldiers (some of whom were Protestant), they sought to conquer Vienna in the name of Allah. In imitation of what St. Pope Pius V had done in the previous century, Blessed Pope Innocent XI formed a Holy League and entrusted the defense of Vienna to the Blessed Virgin Mary. His Holy League was comprised of armies from Poland, Germany, and France.

... Although the city of Vienna was already under siege by the Muslims when [the military commander of the army, King Jan Sobieski of Poland] set out from Warsaw with his 40,000 troops on the 435-mile march to the battlefront, Sobieski's forces marched with determination and resolve, entrusting their mission to Jesus and Mary. In fact, before they began their journey, Jan Sobieski made a detour and brought his entire army before the famous image of Our Lady of Czestochowa, entrusting their cause to the Mother of God. The long march of the army turned into a tremendous rosary procession through fields and towns across Europe. Men prayed it every day, sometimes individually, and other times in large groups. By the time Sobieski's rosary army finally arrived at Vienna, the Muslims had been attacking the city for two months. The Christian forces inside the city were in desperate need of assistance. Other, smaller armies of the Holy League had been fighting against the Muslims in and around the city, but their efforts had not met with much success. The Muslims had caused major damage to the city and were now very close to breaching the city walls.

... On the morning of September 12, 1683 ... Jan Sobieski attended Mass, entrusted his army to the hands of the Virgin Mary, and began his assault against the Muslims. As Sobieski's soldiers [rode] with abandon down the hill toward the Muslim army, they shouted aloud, "Jesus and Mary,

save us!" And Jesus and Mary did save them, as well as the city of Vienna. The Muslims were defeated in a matter of hours. Our Lady of the Rosary had been victorious again! After the battle, King Jan Sobieski related the events of the victory to Pope Innocent XI, describing to the pontiff exactly what had happened that day. He said, "I came, I saw, God conquered!"[5] Upon his return to Poland, Jan Sobieski went immediately to the shrine of Our Lady of Czestochowa on a pilgrimage of thanksgiving and laid the banners captured from the defeated Muslim army before the miraculous image.[6]

In thanksgiving, Pope Innocent XI declared September 12 to be the Feast of the Most Holy Name of Mary for the universal Church. The *Catholic Encyclopedia* reminds us that "We venerate the name of Mary because it belongs to her who is the Mother of God, the holiest of creatures, the Queen of heaven and earth, the Mother of Mercy. The object of the feast is the Holy Virgin bearing the name of *Mirjam* (Mary); the feast commemorates all the privileges given to Mary by God and all the graces we have received through her intercession and mediation."[7]

For each name in this book, I included the feast day for the Marian title to which the name refers, when possible, but for those names that can't be connected to an existing feast, I've offered the Feast of the Most Holy Name of Mary as that name's feast. Indeed, bearers of any of the names in this book can celebrate their name day on September 12, if they so choose.

Names for girls

Though the name Mary was thought to be too holy to be used as a given name in some cultures until the latter half of the second millennium, Catholic parents since have often thought it important to bestow upon their daughters a form of her name, in either the first or middle slot. There's a reason names like Mary Kate and Mary Clare sound very Irish to us; why St. Therese and her sisters and mother all had given names starting with Marie; why Spanish names like Marisol and Italian names like Mariassunta are not uncommon: The traditionally Catholic countries and cultures have loved giving the name of Mary to their daughters.

However, it's telling that, while the name Mary held the number one spot on the American baby name list almost every year from the time the Social Security Administration (SSA) began keeping records in 1880, it was unseated for good by Lisa in 1962 and is currently at number 127, according to the most recent statistics (2016) available from the SSA.[8]

Is such a trend evidence of a decline in interest in naming girls after Mary, or of a decline in a conviction that such a thing is good to do? Or is it the result of the interest many modern American parents have in unusual and creative names?

If the answer is yes to any of the above questions, I hope this list of female Marian names inspires a resurgence in honoring Mary with given and Confirmation names, while still appealing to the sensibilities of those for whom "Mary" just isn't their style.

The names included here come from the many titles of Our Lady; apparitions, events, and places in her life; adjectives used to describe her; and the many forms of the name "Mary" itself. I've included here all the names I could find that referred to Mary, and I added in some entries that may not have ever been used as given names, but which I think are well suited to be so used.

Finally, I used different criteria for forming my list of female names than I did for my list of male names. For example, I did not include in the girls' section the female versions of some of the corresponding male names listed in the boys' section (e.g., John, Joseph), while I did for others (e.g., Clementine, Gabriela). Some male visionaries have a place in the boys' section (e.g., Juan Diego for the apparition at Guadalupe), but I didn't include any female visionaries (e.g., Bernadette and Jacinta for the apparitions at Lourdes and Fátima) unless their names were already Marian (e.g., Lucia as a variant of Lux, Luz). These decisions were made mostly because the girls' section has so many beautiful Marian names that are already being used throughout the world, while the list of male names in honor of Mary is much shorter. They were also made based on "gut-feeling" reasons that made sense to me at the time. That doesn't mean, of course, that, were the proper intention in place (i.e., the intention of honoring Mary through the selection of a certain name), such names couldn't also be given to girls. In fact, the idea of having the proper intention behind the choice of a name is applicable to all of the names in this volume, for even the name "Mary" given only to honor a relative, or only because one likes its sound, is not the same as giving it for the specific purpose of honoring Our Lady.

For each entry, I've included the following information where applicable: name, pronunciation, commentary, nickname(s) (both established, and ones I felt would be possible), variant(s) of the name, feast day(s), and "see also" names (a suggestion to see the entries for other names in the book that might have some connection to that particular entry and/or might contain more information about the Marian connection with that name). Scattered throughout the book are examples of certain names being used in real life, literature, or culture, which is one of my favorite features. Regarding the feast day(s), I've included the feast day of the Marian title or apparition to which the name refers, where appropriate, but not the feast day of any saint who might bear the name, so as to retain the proposed Marian character of each name. (I took a different approach in the boys' section, and included the saints' feast days where applicable.)

Finally, a note about names related to purported apparitions of Our Lady: Only a handful of apparitions have received formal approval from the Church, yet there are many, many names in this book that relate to pious traditions surrounding local apparitions. The inclusion of those names in this book is no comment on their validity; rather, I sought only to present all the names I could find that are bestowed by parents in honor of Our Lady.

Achiropita

Pronunciation: \ ä-kē-ˈrō-pē-tə \

There is an icon of Our Lady in Rossano, Italy called *Madonna della Achiropita* ("Our Lady of Achiropita"). Tradition holds that the image appeared on the wall of the town cathedral in 1140; *achiropita* is Greek for "not made by hands."

Nicknames: Chiro, Kiro, Pita

Variant: Acheropita

Feast day: December 26 (Our Lady of Achiropita)

See also: Tilma

Addolorata

Pronunciation: \ ä-dō-lō-ˈra-ta \

This lovely name comes from the Italian titles *Maria Addolorata* and *Madonna Addolorata*, which refer to Our Lady of Sorrows — Addolorata is an Italian cognate of the Spanish name Dolores (which literally translates as "sorrows").

Nicknames: Ada, Addy, Dolly, Dora, Lola, Lora

Variant: Dolorata, Doloretta, Dolorina

Feast day: September 15 (Our Lady of Sorrows)

See also: Angustias, Dolores, Iris, Ivy, Madonna, Piedad, Pierce (b), Pieta, Simeon (b), Tristan (b)

Ainhoa

Pronunciation: \ 'ī-nō-ə, ī-'nō-ə \

Ainhoa is a city in the Basque region of France, just north of the Spanish border, close to where Our Lady appeared atop a hawthorn (thorn bush) to a shepherd in the 15th century. There is a chapel in Ainhoa dedicated to Our Lady's thorn-bush apparition, where she is known as both *Notre Dame de l'Aubépine* (French for "Our Lady of the Hawthorn") and *Notre Dame d'Aránzazu* (*Aránzazu* comes from the Basque word for "thorn bush"). The name has good usage in the Spanish- and Basque-speaking areas of the world.

Feast day: June 11 (Our Lady of Aránzazu)

See also: Aranza, Hawthorn (b)

Ainhoa in real life, literature, and/or culture
Famous bearers include popular Spanish singer/songwriter Ainhoa Cantalapiedra (known as simply Ainhoa), and Spanish opera soprano Ainhoa Arteta (a native of the Basque region of Spain).

Akita

Pronunciation: \ ə-ˈkē-tə, ä-ˈkē-tə \

Our Lady of Akita is a Marian title referring to apparitions of Our Lady in Akita, Japan in 1973; there is a weeping statue of Our Lady and the miraculous healing of the visionary's deafness associated with the apparitions.

Nicknames: Key, Kiki

Feast day: July 6 (Our Lady of Akita)

See also: Banneux (b), Beauraing (b), Fatima, Guadalupe, Guadalupe (b), Kibeho, Kibeho (b), Knock (b), Lourdes, Salette, Tepeyac (b), Walsingham (b)

Alma

Pronunciation: \ ˈal-mə \

One of Mary's titles is *Alma Redemptoris Mater*, which, being part of a Latin antiphon honoring Our Lady, has been translated into English in several ways by different authors, depending on their intended poetic effect: "Mother of Christ," by Fr. Edward Caswall; "Kindly Mother of the Redeemer," by John Henry Cardinal Newman; "Sweet Mother of Our Saviour Blest," by John Wallace; "Maiden! Mother of Him Who redeemed us," by John Patrick Crichton-Stuart, Third Marquess of Bute; and "gentle, loving bounteous mother," by Thomas Sheehan.[9]

These translations are influenced by the various translations of the term *alma* itself: it is said to be a Hebrew word meaning "young

woman" (married as well as unmarried); it can also come from the Latin *almus*, meaning "nourishing," and the Spanish *alma*, which means "soul."

Feast day: January 1 (Mary, Mother of God)

Almudena

Pronunciation: \ al-mü-ˈdā-na \

Devotion to Nuestra *Señora de la Almudena* ("Our Lady of Almudena") dates to the 11th century, when a Madrid mosque was conquered by Alfonso VI and was renamed for Our Lady (*almudena* is an Arabic word used in this context to refer to Madrid); tradition holds that a miraculous image of Our Lady appeared after the conquest. Our Lady of Almudena is the patroness of Madrid, and St. John Paul II consecrated the Our Lady of Almudena Cathedral in 1993.

Nicknames: Allie, Almu, Dena
Feast day: November 9 (Our Lady of Almudena)

Almudena in real life, literature, and/or culture
Almudena Cid Tostado is a Spanish rhythmic gymnast who competed in the Atlanta, Sydney, Athens, and Beijing Olympics.

Altagracia

Pronunciation: \ äl-ta-ˈgrä-sē-a \

Altagracia is a reference to Our Lady of High Grace (*alta gracia* means "high grace" in Spanish). It refers specifically to a late 15th-/ early 16th-century portrait by an unknown Spanish artist of Our Lady worshiping the newborn Jesus. During his January, 1979 trip to the Dominican Republic, Pope John Paul II crowned the image with a gold and silver tiara, as a gift to Our Lady. Our Lady of High Grace is the patron saint of the Dominican Republic.

Nicknames: Alta (also used as a full name on its own, as a reference to Our Lady of Altagracia), Grace, Gracia, Gracie, Tali

Feast day: January 21 (Our Lady of High Grace)

See also: Grace, Gratian (b)

Amata

Pronunciation: \ ä-ˈmä-tə \

This beautiful name is Latin for "beloved," and Our Lady is referred to as *Mater amata* ("beloved Mother") in the hymn *O Sanctissima*.

Nicknames: Amy, Ammy, Mattie

Variants: Amy (English), Aimée (French), Amada (Spanish)

Feast day: January 1 (Mary, Mother of God)

See also: Amabilis (b), Annabel, Meryt, Morna

Amparo

Pronunciation: \ äm-ˈpä-rō \

Amparo is a Spanish word meaning "refuge, shelter, protection." *Nuestra Señora del Amparo* ("Our Lady of Protection") refers to images of Our Lady in Seville, Spain, and in Puerto La Cruz, Venezuela. *Nuestra Señora de los Desamparados* ("Our Lady of the Abandoned," also translated as "Our Lady of the Forsaken"; *desamparados* refers to those who have the opposite of the "refuge, shelter, protection" to which *amparo* refers) is patroness of the city of Valencia, Spain, and there's a miraculous statue and a confraternity associated with the title as well, established to care for the *desamparados*.

Nicknames: Amy, Pari

Feast days: Second Sunday in May
(Our Lady of the Abandoned
[*Desamparados*], Valencia, Spain)
Second Sunday in November (Our Lady of Amparo, Seville, Spain)
November 8 (Our Lady of Amparo, Venezuela)

See also: Refugio (b)

Ancilla

Pronunciation: \ an-ˈsi-lə, än-ˈchē-la (Italian), än-ˈkē-la (Latin) \

When the Angel Gabriel told Mary of God's plan for her to conceive the Son of God, she replied, "Behold, I am the handmaid of the Lord. May it be done to me according to your word" (Lk 1:38). In Latin, "handmaid of the Lord" is *ancilla Domini*, which is where this lovely name comes from.

Nicknames: Annie, Anna, Cilla

Variants: Ansilla, Anzilla

Feast day: March 25 (Annunciation)

See also: Annunziata, Fiat, Gabriel (b), Gabriela, Nunzio (b)

***Ancilla* in real life, literature, and/or culture**

The official name of Ancilla College in Donaldson, Indiana is Ancilla Domini College, and was established by the Congregation of the Poor Handmaids of Jesus Christ. Additionally, a friend of mine knows a little girl named Ancilla, after Our Lady.

Angela

Pronunciation: \ ˈan-jə-lə \

One of Our Lady's beautiful titles is "Queen of the Angels," so any of the Angel variants can work to honor her.

Nicknames: Angel, Angie, Annie

Variants: Angel (various), Ángeles (Spanish), Angelia (English), Angelica (various), Angelina (various), Angeline (French), Angelique (French, Dutch), Angelita (Spanish), Aniela (Polish), Anielka (Polish)

Feast day: August 2 (Our Lady, Queen of Angels)

See also: Angelo (b), Angelus (b), Seraphim (b), Seraphina

Angel- names in real life and/or culture

For better and worse, the Angel- names are well represented among celebrities, including well-known actresses Anjelica Huston and Angelina Jolie.

In Catholic circles, the American nun and founder of the EWTN TV station was the beloved Mother Angelica — her full religious name was Mother Mary Angelica of the Annunciation, PCPA (Poor Clares of Perpetual Adoration, which is a contemplative Franciscan order of nuns), née Rita Antoinette Rizzo.

Angustias

Pronunciation: \ än-ˈgüs-tē-äs \

The Spanish title *Nuestra Señora de las Angústias* ("Our Lady of Sorrows" or "Our Lady of Anguish"; *angústias* translates as "anguish") can refer specifically to a mysterious statue — similar to the *Pieta* — discovered by fisherman in the 16th century near Ayamonte, Spain, as well as to various churches and other locations where Our Lady is revered under this title.

Nicknames: Angie, Gussie, Tia, Tisa

Feast day: September 15 (Our Lady of Sorrows) Last weekend of September (and often beginning the Wednesday before that) (Our Lady of Sorrows, Granada, Spain)

See also: Addolorata, Dolores, Iris, Ivy, Piedad, Pierce (b), Pieta, Simeon (b), Tristan (b)

Anna

Pronunciation: \ ˈan-nə, ä-na \

There are three different connections to Our Lady through the name Anna. First, Our Lady's Magnificat (Lk 1:46-55) mirrors the Song of Hannah in the Old Testament (1 Sam 2:1-10) (Anna is the Greek and Latin variant of the Hebrew "Hannah"). Second, the prophetess Anna in the Bible was, with Simeon, one who recognized the Baby Jesus as the Messiah when Mary and Joseph brought Him to the temple for the Presentation (Fourth Joyful Mystery of the Rosary; Lk 2:36-38). It was during this time that Simeon prophesied that Mary's heart would be pierced by a sword (Lk 2:25-35). Third, Mary's mother is traditionally revered under the name St. Ann(e), a variant of Anna, which means "favor" or "grace" — such apt meanings for the name of the mother of Our Lady and the grandmother of Our Lord!

Nicknames: Anita, Annie, Nan, Nancy

Variants: Áine (Irish), Ana (various), Anaïs (various), Ani (various), Anica (Croatian, Slovene), Anika (Slovene), Anita (various), Anja (various), Anke (German), Ann (English), Anne (French), Annetta (Italian), Annette (French), Annika (Swedish), Annushka (Russian), Anya (Russian), Chana (Hebrew), Channah (Hebrew), Hana (various), Hannah (Hebrew)

Feast days: February 2 (Presentation of the Baby Jesus in the Temple, also known as Candlemas, as well as the Purification of Mary)
December 8 (Immaculate Conception),
September 8 (Birth of Our Lady)

See also: Anselm (b), Candelaria, Candelario (b), Grace, Joachim (b), Pierce (b), Purificación, Simeon (b)

Annabel

Pronunciation: \ˈan-ə-bel \

According to various sources, the name Annabel arose in Scotland in the Middle Ages as a variant of Amabel, which comes from the Latin *amabilis*, meaning "lovable," and is part of the Marian title *Mater Amabilis* ("Mother Most Amiable" or "Mother Most Lovable"). Additionally, Annabel(le) has come to be associated with the Ann- names, and the French meaning of *belle* as "beautiful" adds another layer of meaning.

Nicknames: Anna, Annie, Belle, Bella

Variants: Amabilia, Anabel (Spanish), Anabela (Portuguese), Annabel (English, Dutch), Annabella (English, Italian), Arabel (English, Scottish), Arabelle (English, French), Arabella (English, Scottish), Mabel/Mable (English), Mabell (Spanish), Mabella (English), Mabelle (English, French), Maybelle (English), Maybelline (English)

Feast day: January 1 (Mary, Mother of God)

See also: Amabilis (b), Amata, Anna, Meryt, Morna

***Mabel* and *Maybelline* in real life, literature, and/or culture**
In the sitcom "Mad About You," the main characters named their daughter Mabel, because each letter of "Mabel" can stand for the phrase "Mothers Always Bring Extra Love." I'm sure the show's writers had no intention of the name referring to Our Lady, but that

doesn't mean *you* can't have that intention! Such a meaning adds a fun — and seriously Marian — extra layer to the name Mabel.

While Maybelline has a beautiful, dainty, French feel, beware of its very strong overriding association with the cosmetics brand Maybelline and its well-known tagline.

Annunziata

Pronunciation: \ än-nün-ˈtsyä-tä \

Italian for "annunciation," Annunziata refers to the appearance of the Angel Gabriel to Our Lady, when he announced to her that she'd been chosen by God to conceive and bear His Son. The Annunciation is the first Joyful Mystery of the Rosary.

Nicknames: Ana, Anita, Anna, Annie, Nunzia, Nunziatina

Variants: Anunciación (Spanish), Annunciata (Italian)

Feast day: March 25 (Annunciation)

See also: Ancilla, Fiat, Gabriel (b), Gabriela, Nunzio (b)

Aparecida

Pronunciation:\ ə-ˌpä-rā-ˈsē-də \

Tradition holds that in a small town in Brazil in 1717, fishermen prayed to Our Lady of the Immaculate Conception for a good catch. They cast their nets and brought up, separately, the head and body of a clay

statue of Our Lady of the Immaculate Conception, and afterward they caught an abundance of fish. They named the statue *Nossa Senhora Aparecida* ("Our Lady of Aparecida"; *aparecida* means "appeared"), and under this title Our Lady is patroness of Brazil by a decree of Pope Pius XI issued on July 16, 1930.

Nicknames: Ara, Ari, Cida

Feast day: October 12 (Our Lady of Aparecida)

See also: Immaculata, Concepción

Araceli

Pronunciation:\ ä-rä-ˈsel-lē (Spanish — Latin America), ä-rä-ˈthel-lē (Spanish — Spain), ä-rä-ˈchel-lē (Italian, Latin)

This beautiful name comes from Our Lady's title *Ara Caeli* (or *Coeli*): "Altar of Heaven." Under this title she is patroness of Lucena, Spain. There is also the beautiful Basilica of Santa Maria in Aracoeli in Rome, at which St. Helena is buried.

Nicknames: Ara, Ari, Celi

Variant: Aracoeli (Latin)

Feast day: March 25 (Annunciation)

See also: Caeli, Celeste, Celestine (b)

Aranza

Pronunciation: \ ä-ˈrän-zä \

The Basque word *arantza* means "thorn bush" or "hawthorn," and the name Aranza and its many variants refer to an apparition of Our Lady to a shepherd named Rodrigo de Baltzátegui in the Basque region of Spain on June 11, 1469. Mary appeared holding the Infant Jesus, to which Rodrigo exclaimed, *"¡Arantza Zu! ¡Arantza Zu!"* which is Basque for "You among the thorns!" After she relayed her message to Rodrigo (to build a shrine on the site) and returned to Heaven, Rodrigo discovered a stone statue of Mary holding Baby Jesus atop a thorn tree. She is known in English as Our Lady of Thorns, Our Lady of the Thorn Tree, and Our Lady of Aránzazu, and in French as *Notre Dame de l'Aubepine and Notre Dame d'Aránzazu.*

Nicknames: Ari, Ranza

Variants: Arancha, Arantxa, Arantza, Arántzazu, Aranza, Aránzazu, Arrántzazu (Arancha, Arantxa, Arantza, and Aranza are also traditional nicknames for Arántzazu, Aránzazu, and Arrántzazu)

Feast day: June 11 (Our Lady of Aránzazu)

See also: Ainhoa, Hawthorn (b)

Aranza in real life, literature, and/or culture

When the SSA released its 2014 name statistics, many were surprised to see that Aranza shared the spotlight with Montserrat/Monserrat in being the fastest-rising girls' names in America. They were boosted by use on *telenovelas* (Latin soap operas), but Aranza's originating use is Marian through and through.

Assumpta

Pronunciation: \ə-ˈsəm(p)-tə\

Assumpta is from the Latin for "assumption," referring to the Assumption of Our Blessed Lady into Heaven, body and soul (Fourth Glorious Mystery of the Rosary).

Nicknames: Amy, Sue, Susie

Variants: Assunta (Italian), Asunción (Spanish)

Feast Day: August 15 (Assumption)

See also: Assunto (b), Susanna

Assunta in real life, literature, and/or culture

I was due with my second baby on the Feast of the Assumption, August 15. When the mother of a friend discovered the due date, she said, "If you have a girl, you should name her …" I was sure (I, ahem, *assumed!*) that she was about to say "Assunta," "Assumpta," or something similar, but instead she came out with "Susan!"

Susan? It turns out that many people of Italian descent have used the name Susan as the English "translation" of the common Italian name Assunta. A quick Internet search revealed that it's not uncommon for American women with the given name Assunta to go by Susan.

As far as I can tell, there's no etymological connection between Assunta and Susan, but my guess is that it may have evolved because of the similarity in sound between the two. Regardless, it's a lovely thing for Susans everywhere to now know of this particular Marian layer to their name, especially if they're Italian!

Aurea

Pronunciation: \ ˈȯr-ē-ə, ˈau̇-rē-ä (Italian, Latin, Spanish) \

Aurea is Latin for "golden," as in the golden crown Our Lady is depicted wearing in her images as Queen; the golden roses she had on her feet in her apparition at Lourdes; her title of "Virgin with the Golden Heart," because her heart appeared golden during some of her apparitions at Beauraing; and her title "Golden Rose, Queen of Ireland" in the beautiful song "Lady of Knock" by the Irish singer Dana. In addition, *Rosa Aurea* is the name of an 1886 list of Rosary indulgences by Fr. Thomas Maria Leikes, OP, which referenced over 200 "official papal documents on the rosary ... It remains an invaluable resource for any historian of the rosary."[10]

Nicknames: Auri, Rea, Ria

Feast day: September 12 (Most Holy Name of Mary)

See also: Beauraing (b), Candace, Corona, Incoronata, Knock (b), Lourdes, Marigold, Regina, Reina, Reginald (b), Rose

Aurora

Pronunciation: \ ə-ˈrȯr-ə, ȯ-ˈrȯr-ə, ˈau̇-ˈrȯr-ə (Italian, Latin, Spanish) \

Aurora is Latin for "dawn," which gives the name its Marian character. The Venerable Mary of Agreda referred to Our Lady as the "resplendent Aurora Mary" in her *Mystical City of God* — such a lovely description![11] St. Bonaventure also used "Aurora" in reference to Mary 35 times in his *Mirror of the Blessed Virgin Mary*, and the *Little Office of the Blessed Virgin Mary* includes a reference to Our Lady as *aurora* in the closing prayer for Vespers.[12]

Nicknames: Aura, Auri, Ro, Rory

Variants: Aurore (French), Dawn (English)

Feast day: September 12 (Most Holy Name of Mary)

See also: Danica

Aurora in real life, literature, and/or culture
I once read on a baby name discussion board about twins named
Aurora and Therese — what beautiful Catholic names! The parents
used the \ tə-ˈrēs \ pronunciation for Therese, and nicknamed the girls
Rory and Reese. How darling!

You might also remember that Princess Aurora is Sleeping Beauty's
real name in the animated Disney version of the story.

Auxilio

Pronunciation: \ ȯg-ˈzi-lē-ō, au̇k-ˈzi-lē-ō \

Meaning "help" in Spanish, Auxilio is a feminine name in Spanish and
a masculine name in Portuguese. It refers to the Marian title *Maria
Auxiliadora* ("Mary the Helper," also known as "Our Lady, Help of
Christians"). In fact, the combination "Maria Auxiliadora" is not an
uncommon given name, nor is Maria Auxilio.

Nicknames: Zilia, Zilio, Zillie

Feast day: May 24 (Our Lady, Help of Christians)

See also: Auxilio (b), Perpetua, Socorro

Ave

Pronunciation: \ ˈä-vā \

Ave is from the Latin for "hail," as in "Hail, Mary" (*Ave Maria*; Hail Marys have sometimes been referred to as *aves*); also, there's the hymn *Ave Maris Stella* ("Hail, Star of the Sea"), which includes this amazing verse:

> O! By Gabriel's Ave,
> Uttered long ago,
> Eva's name reversing,
> Established peace below.[13]

Though not common as a given name, its similarity to the popular name Ava makes this feasible as a real option. The reference to Our Lady is unquestionably cemented if Maria is paired with either Ave or Ava as a middle name.

Feast day: March 25 (Annunciation)

See also: Annunziata, Eve, Gabriel (b), Gabriela, Hailemariam, Maris, Nunzio (b), Stella

Azucena

Pronunciation: \ ä-sü-ˈsä-nä (Spanish — Latin America), ä-thü-ˈthä-nä (Spanish — Spain) \

This name refers to a lovely flower known as the Madonna lily (*Lilium candidum*, also known as the Annunciation lily, Virgin lily, and Mary lily), and shares the same root as Susanna, which means both "lily" and "rose."

Nicknames: Azu, Cena, Susie, Zuzu

Feast days: January 1 (Mary, Mother of God)
March 25 (Annunciation)

See also: Annunziata, Lily, Madonna,
Nunzio (b), Rose, Susanna, Virginia

Beata

Pronunciation: \ bē-ä-tə, bā-ˈä-tə\

Beata is from the Latin *beatus*, meaning "blessed, fortunate, supreme-ly happy." Our Lady is called *beata* in certain circumstances, such as in the Latin for "Assumption of the Blessed Virgin Mary" (*Assumptione Beatae Mariae Virginis*).

Nicknames: Bea, Bee, Betty

Variant: Behati

Feast day: March 25 (Annunciation)

See also: Beatrix, Benedict (b), Benedicta, Gwenfair, Mairwen

Beata and Behati in real life, literature, and/or culture
Though fairly rare in the United States, Beata is well represented elsewhere, especially in Eastern Europe; its BehindTheName.com entry has more than a dozen notable Beatas listed in the comments from Poland, the Czech Republic, Slovakia, and elsewhere.

An intriguing name that's said to possibly be a variant of Beata is Behati, borne by the Namibian model Behati Prinsloo, wife of Maroon 5 front man Adam Levine. Her dad reported that her name means "blessing."[14]

Beatrix

Pronunciation: \ ˈbē-triks, ˈbē-ə-triks, ˈbā-ə-triks \

As the word *beatrix* in Latin means "she who blesses, makes happy, delights," the name Beatrix can easily refer to Our Lady, who blesses us all and is the Cause of Our Joy (*Causa Nostrae Laetitiae*)![15]

Nicknames: Bea, Bee, Betty, Bex, Tris, Trixie

Variants: Beatrice (Italian, French), Beatriz (Spanish), Bettrys (Welsh)

Feast day: December 2 (Our Lady of Joy, also known as Our Lady of Liesse)

See also: Beata, Benedict (b), Benedicta, Laetitia, Leeson (b), Liesse, Maeve

***Beatrix* in real life, literature, and/or culture**
An interesting fact is that writer Beatrix Potter (of *Peter Rabbit* fame) was actually named Helen Beatrix.

Begoña

Pronunciation: \ be-ˈgō-nyə \

Pronounced just like the name of the begonia flower (which serves to add a pretty floral feel to this name), Begoña comes from the Spanish

Marian title *Nuestra Señora de Begoña* ("Our Lady of Begoña"), refer-ring to the Spanish municipality of Begoña (which was incorporated into the city of Bilbao in the province of Biscay in 1925) in which Our Lady appeared in the 16th century.

Nicknames: Bea, Bega, Nonie

Feast day: October 11 (Feast of Our Lady of Begoña)

Belén

Pronunciation: \ be-'len \

The lovely name Belén is Spanish for "Bethlehem," and the Marian connection is twofold. First, the title "Our Lady of Bethlehem" (*Nuestra Señora de Belén* in Spanish). Secondly, the name of Bethlehem comes from the Hebrew for "house of bread" — with Jesus being the Bread of Life and Our Lady his dwelling place until birth, it seems an apt description for her.

Variants: Belém (Portuguese), Bethlehem (English)

Feast day: December 25 (Our Lady of Bethlehem)

See also: Nazaret, Nazario (b)

Benedicta

Pronunciation: \ be-nə-'dik-tə \

From the Latin for "blessed," Mary is called *benedicta* in the Latin form of the Hail Mary.

Nicknames: Beca, Benny, Betty, Bonnie, Neddy, Nettie

Variants: Benedetta (Italian), Benedita (Portuguese), Benita (Spanish)

Feast day: March 25 (Annunciation)

See also: Beata, Beatrix, Benedict (b), Gwenfair, Mairwen

Biancamaria

Pronunciation: \ ˈbyäŋ-ka-ma-ˈrē-a \

Bianca is Italian for "white," and in Italy, Bianca Maria or Biancmaria is a name given to baby girls in honor of Our Lady of the Snows.

Nicknames: Bee, Bree, Bria

Variants: Bianca Maria, Bianca-Maria

Feast day: August 5 (Our Lady of the Snows)

See also: Gwenfair, Ivory, Ivory (b), Mairwen, Meritxell, Nieves

Bianca Maria in real life, literature, and/or culture
American actress Bianca Kajlich's given name is Bianca Maria Kajlich. She has appeared on TV shows such as "Rules of Engagement," "Boston Public," and "Dawson's Creek."

Blue

Pronunciation: \ blü \

The color blue has long been associated with Our Lady. In her apparitions, she's often wearing blue (e.g., at Guadalupe she wore a blue mantle; at Lourdes she had on a blue sash); "The Blue Madonna" is a beautiful painting by Carlo Dolci (17th century); and Ven. Fulton Sheen popularized the poem "Lovely Lady Dressed in Blue" by Mary Dixon Thayer. The bluebell flowers (*Campanula rotundifolia*) have also been known as Our Lady's Thimble.

Variants: Azul (Spanish), Blau (German), Bleu (French), Blu (Italian)

Feast day: September 12 (Most Holy Name of Mary)

See also: Blue (b), Fulton, Guadalupe, Guadalupe (b), Lourdes, Madonna, Mantle (b), Veil

Blue in real life, literature, and/or culture

Performers Beyoncé and Jay Z named their little girl Blue Ivy, and actors John Travolta and Kelly Preston gave their daughter the French variant of this for a middle name: Ella Bleu. For an ultra-Marian combination, check out Spice Girl Geri Halliwell's daughter's name: Bluebell Madonna!

Caeli

Pronunciation: \ ˈchā-lē (Latin), ˈkā-lē (English) \

Caeli is Latin for "heaven," and can be seen in the Marian titles *Ara Caeli* ("Altar of Heaven") and *Regina Caeli* ("Queen of Heaven"). Its similarity to such current favorites as Kaylee/Caylee, Caley, Kiley, Kayla, and Kyla, especially if the pronunciation \ ˈkā-lē \ is used, makes this a good pick for those who like the current trends in names, but still want to honor Our Lady. The pronunciation \ ˈchā-lē \ has a more old-school Catholic feel to it, as it's the Church Latin (or Ecclesiastical Latin) pronunciation.

Variant: Coeli

Feast days: March 25 (Annunciation)
August 22 (Queenship of Mary)

See also: Araceli, Candace, Celeste, Celestine (b),
Regina, Reginald (b), Reina

Cana

Pronunciation: \ ˈkā-nə \

This name refers to the Wedding Feast at Cana, at which Jesus performed his first miracle, changing water into wine because his mother asked him to (Second Luminous Mystery of the Rosary). I've always

loved this example of Our Lady's love for us and her intercession on our behalf.

Feast day: January 1 (Mary, Mother of God)

Candace

Pronunciation: \ ˈkan-dis, kan-ˈdā-sē, ˈkan-di-sē \

This biblical name, mentioned in Acts 8:27, was the title of the queens of Ethiopia. It's said to mean "queen mother" in Cushitic, which perfectly describes Our Lady.

Nicknames: Caddy, Cadie, Cady, Cana, Candi, Candie, Candy, Casey, Dacey, Daisy

Variants: Candice, Candis, Candyce, Kandace, Kandice

Feast days: January 1 (Mary, Mother of God)
August 22 (Queenship of Mary)

See also: Daisy, Madonna, Regina, Reginald (b), Reina, Theotokos (b)

***Candace* and *Candice* in real life, literature, and/or culture**
Actress Candice Bergen (b. 1946) played Murphy Brown in the TV show of the same name. Actress Candace Cameron Bure (b. 1976) made a name for herself as D.J. Tanner on the TV show "Full House," and also competed on "Dancing with the Stars" in 2014. A character named Candace went by "Caddy" in William Faulkner's novel *The Sound and the Fury*.

Candelaria

Pronunciation: \ kän-də-ˈlä-ryə, kan-də-ˈler-ē-ə \

Candelaria is the Spanish word for Candlemas, the feast that commemorates both the Presentation of the Baby Jesus in the Temple (Fourth Joyful Mystery), and also the purification of Our Lady after having given birth, and has traditionally been bestowed in her honor.

Nicknames: Cande, Candela, Candelas, Candie, Candy, Della, Lara, Ria

Feast Day: February 2 (Candlemas, also known as the Feast of the Presentation of the Baby Jesus in the Temple, as well as the Feast of the Purification of Mary)

See also: Candelario (b), Purificación

Carmel

Pronunciation: \ ˈkär-məl \

The name Carmel is from the Marian title "Our Lady of Mount Carmel," after which the Carmelite Order takes its name. Carmel comes from the Hebrew for "garden," and is the name of a mountain in the Holy Land featured in the Old Testament book of First Kings, chapter 18. In this chapter, the prophet Elijah instructed his servant to look out to the sea from Mount Carmel and report what he saw there; six times the servant reported there was nothing to see, and Elijah sent him to look again. After the seventh time, the servant told Elijah, "There is a cloud as small as a man's hand rising from the sea" (1 Kings 18:44). Carmelite tradition holds that Elijah understood this cloud to be a symbol of the Virgin Mother who would bear the Messiah, as foretold

in the book of Isaiah: "Therefore the Lord himself will give you a sign; the young woman, pregnant and about to bear a son, shall name him Emmanuel" (Is 7:14).

Nicknames: Callie, Cammie, Cammy, Cara, Cari, Carly, Carmie, Caro, Carrie, Ella, Ellie, Lina, Mel, Mela, Melly, Millie

Variants: Carmela (Italian, Spanish), Carmelina (Italian), Carmelita (Spanish), Carmella (English), Carmen (various), Carmina (Italian, Spanish)

Feast day: July 16 (Our Lady of Mount Carmel)

See also: Carmelo (b), Elijah (b), Stock (b)

Carmen **in real life, literature, and/or culture**
The opera *Carmen* by Georges Bizet is well known.

Catena

Pronunciation: \ kä-ˈtā-nä \

Madonna della Catena and *Maria Santissima della Catena* are Italian appellations referring to Our Lady of the Chain, patron of slaves and prisoners, after a 14th-century miracle in Palermo, Sicily, in which three men who had been wrongly convicted and chained to await their execution were set free in the night — their chains broken — by Our Lady. As with so many discussed in this book, this appears to be a hyper-local devotion, with many towns in Sicily and Italy having their own devotions and feast days to Our Lady of the Chain.

Feast days: Various dates from January to July,
specific to different towns in Sicily and Italy

Celeste

Pronunciation: \ sə-ˈlest, chə-ˈles-tā (Italian, Latin), sə-ˈles-tā (Spanish) \

From the Latin *caelestis*, meaning "heavenly" (as you can see from the word "celestial"), Celeste refers to Our Lady in her titles "Queen of Heaven" and "Altar of Heaven." It's a feminine name in English, French, and Italian, and a masculine name in French and Italian as well.

Nicknames: Cece, Cel, Celly

Variant: Celestine

Feast days: March 25 (Annunciation)
August 22 (Queenship of Mary)

See also: Araceli, Caeli, Candace, Celestine (b),
Regina, Reginald (b), Reina

Charity

Pronunciation: \ ˈcher-ə-tē, ˈcha-rə-tē \

The word "charity" comes from the Latin *caritas* meaning "generous love," which comes from the Latin *carus*, meaning "dear, beloved." Our Lady of Charity (*Nuestra Señora de la Virgen de la Caridad* in Spanish) is one of Mother Mary's many titles, revered around the world, and as such she was designated Patroness of Cuba by Pope Benedict XV in 1916; her shrine was elevated to the status of basilica in 1977 by Pope

Paul VI; and Pope St. John Paul II crowned the image again as queen and patroness of Cuba in 1998 (that particular rendition of Our Lady of Charity is also known as Our Lady of Charity of El Cobre, or simply Our Lady of El Cobre, after the town of El Cobre near Santiago, Cuba, near where a statue of Our Lady of Charity miraculously appeared in the early 1600s; she is affectionately referred to as Cachita).

Variants: Caridad (Spanish), Carita (Swedish), Caritas (Latin), Karita (Swedish)

Feast day: September 8 (Our Lady of Charity)

See also: Faith, Grace, Hope

Civita

Pronunciation: \ ˈchē-vē-tä \

This given name is from the Italian title *Madonna della Civita* ("Our Lady of the City"), referring to an image of Our Lady whose shrine in Itri is one of the oldest in Italy. Tradition holds that it was painted by St. Luke himself. Though records of it date back to the eighth century, it had disappeared and was found on Mount Civita by a deaf shepherd whose hearing and speech were restored in the presence of the painting.

Nicknames: Civi, Vita

Feast day: July 21 (Madonna della Civita)

See also: Luke

Clementine

Pronunciation: \ ˈkle-mən-tīn, ˈkle-mən-tēn \

This is the feminine form of the male name Clement, which comes from the Latin *clemens*, which means "merciful" or "gentle," and is used as an adjective for Our Lady in the prayer and song *Salve Regina* ("Hail Holy Queen").

Nicknames: Clem, Clemmie, Emmy, Ina, Minnie, Tina

Variants: Clemence (English), Clemency (English), Clementina (various), Klementina (Croatian), Klementyna (Polish)

Feast day: September 24 (Our Lady of Mercy, also known as Our Lady of Ransom)

See also: Clement (b), Mercedes, Mercer (b), Mercy, Misericordia, Ransom (b)

Concepción

Pronunciation: \ kōn-sep-ˈsyȯn \

This means "conception" in Spanish, and refers to the Immaculate Conception of Our Lady:

> In the Constitution *Ineffabilis Deus* of 8 December, 1854, Pius IX pronounced and defined that the Blessed Virgin Mary "in the first instance of her conception, by a singular privilege and grace granted by God, in view of the merits of Jesus Christ, the Saviour of the human race, was preserved exempt from all stain of original sin."[16]

Nicknames: Chita, Concha, Conchita, Etta, Etty

Variants: Concepta (English, Irish), Concetta (Italian), Concettina (Italian)

Feast day: December 8 (Immaculate Conception)

See also: Beauraing (b), Immaculata, Kolbe (b), Lourdes, Maximilian (b)

Conseja

Pronunciation: \ kȯn-ˈsā-ha \

This name is derived from the Spanish for Our Lady of Good Counsel (*Nuestra Señora del Buen Consejo*). There is a fourth-century church in Italy called St. Mary, Mother of Good Counsel, and there's a beautiful image of the Madonna and Child at Genazzano, Italy referred to as Our Lady of Good Counsel (*Madonna del Buon Consiglio* in Italian) to which miracles have been attributed. Pope Paul II approved devotion to Our Lady of Good Counsel in the 15th century; the Augustinians and Jesuits have a special devotion to her; and Pope Leo XIII added "Mother of Good Counsel" to the Litany of Loreto in 1903.

Nicknames: Connie, Seja

Variant: Consilia (Italian)

Feast days: April 26 (Our Lady of Good Counsel, universal)
April 25 (Our Lady of Good Counsel, in Genazzano, Italy)

Consolata

Pronunciation: \ kän-sò-ˈlä-ta \

Italian for "consolation," this comes from the Italian Marian title *Maria Consolata*, known in English as Our Lady of Consolation, Our Lady Consolata, and the Consolata.

This title of Our Lady is an ancient one, referring to Mary's role as a loving mother who embraces us especially in times of hardship. Specifically, it refers to an icon of Our Lady holding the Infant Jesus, the painting of which tradition attributes to St. Luke, and which had been in Turin for hundreds of years before Turin was laid to ruin by civil war in the 11th century, and the image of Our Lady Consolata was buried among the rubble and forgotten.

In the beginning of the 12th century, a blind Frenchman had a vision in a dream in which he saw, buried in the ruins of a church, a painting of Our Lady. He understood that the church was in Turin, and that his efforts would result in Our Lady again being honored in that spot. Our Lady also promised to restore his sight.

The man went to Turin, and effected the excavation of the site. Indeed, first the ruins of the chapel were found, and then the undamaged image of Our Lady Consolata. A large shrine was built on the site, and many blessings were poured out upon the city. To this day, the inhabitants of the city of Turin have a great devotion to the Consolata.

Nicknames: Connie, Lata, Lottie, Sola

Variants: Consuela (Spanish), Consuelo (Spanish)

Feast day: June 20 (Our Lady of Consolation)

See also: Consuelo, Luke (b)

Consuelo

Pronunciation: \ kän-ˈswā-lō \

Spanish for "consolation," Consuelo comes from the Spanish Marian title *Nuestra Señora del Consuelo* ("Our Lady of Consolation").

Nicknames: Chelo, Connie

Variants: Consuela (Spanish), Consolata (Italian)

Feast day: June 20 (Our Lady of Consolation)

See also: Consolata

Cora

Pronunciation: \ ˈkōr-ə \

Though not traditionally used as a Marian name (despite its likely origin as a form of the Greek *kore*, meaning "maiden," which is a great Marian meaning), I know of several families who have used or considered Cora because of its similarity to the Latin *cor*, meaning "heart," and given in honor of the Immaculate Heart of Mary. Pope Pius XII consecrated the world to the Immaculate Heart of Mary, which St. John Paul II renewed in 1984 and 2000.

Nicknames: Cori, Corie, Corrie, Cory

Variants: Coretta (English), Corina (various), Corinna (various), Corinne (English, French), Kora (German), Korina (Greek), Korinna (Greek)

Feast day: Saturday following the Solemnity of the Sacred Heart of Jesus, which is celebrated 19 days after Pentecost (Immaculate Heart of Mary)

See also: Beauraing (b), Immaculata

Corona

Pronunciation: \ kə-ˈrō-nə \

Corona means "crown" in Latin, and refers to the Crowning of Our Lady, also known as the Coronation (Fifth Glorious Mystery of the Rosary).

Nicknames: Cora, Cori, Rona, Nona, Nonie

Feast day: August 22 (Queenship of Mary)

See also: Aurea, Candace, Incoronata, Marigold, Regina, Reina, Reginald (b)

Corona in real life, literature, and/or culture
As lovely and meaningful as this name is, it's good to be aware of the fact that there's a brand of Mexican beer called Corona, which is well known in the U.S.

Cruz

Pronunciations: \ ˈkrüs (Spanish — Latin America),
ˈkrüth (Spanish — Spain), ˈkrüz (English) \

This Spanish word for "cross" is used for both boys and girls, and in a Marian sense refers to Our Lady at the foot of the Cross. It's also added to Maria to form the traditional feminine name Maricruz.

Variants: Croix (French), Cruzita (Spanish), Maricruz (Spanish)

Feast day: March 31 (Our Lady of the Holy Cross)

See also: Addolorata, Angustias, Cruz (b), Dolores, Iris, Ivy, John (b), Piedad, Pierce (b), Pieta, Simeon (b), Tristan (b)

D

Daisy

Pronunciation: \ ˈdā-zē \

The common daisy flower (*Bellis perennis*) has also been known as Mary's flower or Mary-Loves, and the oxeye daisy (*chrysanthemum leucanthemum*) has also been known as Mary's Star. There are two beautiful legends associated with the latter flower — one is that when the Wise Men arrived in Bethlehem, they looked for a sign to let them know where the Holy Family was, and an oxeye daisy — looking like the star that led them to Bethlehem — was growing by the door of the holy stable; the other is that a cluster of them was growing in front of the manger, also reminiscent of the Christmas star. An added layer of Marian meaning can be added to Daisy in the sense that it has occasionally been used as a nickname for Candace (one traditional English pronunciation of Candace is \ kan-ˈdā-sē \, which explains the Daisy connection), which originates from the Cushitic word for "queen mother."

Daisy is also a traditional nickname for Margaret — the French word for the daisy flower is *marguerite*, which is the same as the French form of Margaret.

Feast day: September 12 (Most Holy Name of Mary)

See also: Candace, Pearl

Daisy in real life, literature, and/or culture
Though neither the title character in Henry James' *Daisy Miller*, nor

the character of Daisy Buchanan in F. Scott Fitzgerald's *The Great Gatsby*, are virtuous women, the name Daisy has had good usage in the U.S. as a given name since the SSA began keeping track.

Danica

Pronunciation: \ ˈda-ni-ka, dä-nē-tsä (Slovak) \

Danica is a Slavic word meaning "morning star," which is one of the titles of Our Lady in the Litany of Loreto.

Nicknames: Dani, Nica, Nicki

Variant: Danika

Feast day: September 12 (Most Holy Name of Mary)

See also: Aurora

***Danica* in real life, literature, and/or culture**
Danica McKellar played Winnie Cooper on the popular TV show "The Wonder Years," and Danica Patrick is a highly successful American race car driver.

Demaris

Pronunciation: \ də-ˈmer-iss, də-ˈmär-is \

I've seen it said in several places that this name means "of Mary," and its usage as such makes it good enough for me as a Marian name. It's similar to the Latin *de mari*, meaning "from the sea," and *maris*, meaning "of (belonging to) the sea," both of which can be connected to the Marian title *Stella Maris* ("Star of the Sea").

Demaris is similar in appearance and pronunciation to the name Damaris, which, according to the academic sources, likely originated from the Greek for "calf, heifer, girl," though I've also seen "gentle" and "gentle girl" given as meanings on more than one site. It's the name of a woman who was converted by St. Paul in the Acts of the Apostles (17:34), but I know a family who uses this spelling to mean "of (belonging to) Mary," in which case it might be thought of as a variant of Demaris.

Nicknames: Demi, Mari, Maris, Mary

Variant: Damaris

Feast day: September 12 (Most Holy Name of Mary)

See also: Mariae, Marina, Maris, Stella

Damaris in real life, literature, and/or culture
Though \ ˈdam-ə-ris \ is the pronunciation seemingly preferred by academic sources, Damaris Phillips is a famous "Damaris," who pronounces her name \ də-ˈmer-is \. She is past winner of the Food Network's "Food Network Star" program, and currently stars on her own Food Network show, "Southern at Heart."

Despina

Pronunciation: \ des-ˈpē-nə, ˈdes-pē-nə \

This common Greek name, meaning "lady," is also used to refer to Our Lady. According to the Greek Names website, girls and unmarried women named Despina or its variant Despoina celebrate their name day on November 21, while married women so named celebrate their name day on August 15.[17]

Nicknames: Ania, Depy, Des, Desi, Despo, Nia, Pepi, Pegky, Peny, Zepo

Variant: Despoina

Feast days: August 15 (Assumption)
November 21 (Presentation of Mary)

See also: Assumpta, Assunto (b), Madonna, Matrona, Presentación

Dimanche

Pronunciation: \ dē-ˈmȯnsh \

Notre Dame du Dimanche ("Our Lady of Sunday") is the name of Our Lady as she appeared to a winemaker in 1873 in the southern French community of Saint-Bauzille-de-la-Sylve. It was a Sunday, and the man was working in his vineyard; Our Lady's message to him was, "You must not work on Sundays."

Nicknames: Dee, Dima

Variants: Demange (French), Dominga (Spanish), Sunday (English)

Feast day: June 8 (Our Lady of Sunday)

See also: Dominic (b)

Sunday in real life, literature, and/or culture

Though Dimanche is listed as a first name on Nameberry and in the Behind the Name database, I couldn't find any examples of it as a first name in real life. However, Sunday has current usage: One of the daughters of actress Nicole Kidman and singer Keith Urban is named Sunday Rose.

Dolores

Pronunciation: \ də-ˈlȯr-is \

Dolores is, in origin, a Spanish name, from the Marian title *Nuestra Señora de los Dolores* ("Our Lady of Sorrows"; she's also known as "Our Lady of Piety"), and it refers to the Seven Sorrows (or "Dolors") of Our Lady.

A beautiful hymn to her sorrows is the *Stabat Mater* or *Stabat Mater Dolorosa* ("The Sorrowful Mother Stood"), traditionally sung during Mass for the feast of Our Lady of Sorrows.

Nicknames: Dolly, Dory, Ivy, Lola, Lolita

Variants: Delores, Deloris, Dolorosa

Feast Day: September 15 (Our Lady of Sorrows)

See also: Addolorata, Angustias, Iris, Ivy, Lola, Piedad, Pierce (b), Pieta, Simeon (b), Tristan (b)

***Lolita* in real life, literature, and/or culture**
Though Lolita is a traditional nickname for Dolores, one should be
aware that it currently has a strong sexual connotation due to the
character by the same name in Vladimir Nabokov's 1955
novel *Lolita*.

Dulcie

Pronunciation: \ ˈdül-sē, ˈdül-sē \

Originating from the Latin *dulcis*, meaning "sweet," Dulcie makes
reference to the *dulce nombre de María* — "the sweet name of Mary."
The adjective *dulcis* is itself also used to describe Our Lady in the last
line of the hymn *Salve Regina: "O clemens, O pia, O dulcis Virgo Maria!"*

Variants: Dolcie (English), Dulce (Portuguese, Spanish), Dulcia
(Spanish), Dulcina (Spanish), Dulcinea (Spanish), Dulcinia,
Dulcis (Latin), Dulcy (English)

Feast day: September 12 (Most Holy Name of Mary)

See also: Dowson (b)

Dulcinea in real life, literature, and/or culture

The protagonist's imaginary love interest in the Spanish classic *Don Quixote*, by Miguel de Cervantes (himself a soldier for the faith, having fought and been severely wounded at the Battle of Lepanto), is named Dulcinea del Toboso.[18]

Edelweiss

Pronunciation: \ ˈā-dəl-vīs, ˈā-dəl-wīs \

The lovely white flower *Leontopodium alpinum* is better known as *edelweiss*, a German word combining the elements "noble" and "white." The flower has also been called Purity of Mary.

Nicknames: Ada, Edel

Feast day: October 16 (Purity of the Blessed Virgin Mary)

See also: Biancamaria, Immaculata, Pureza

Edelweiss in real life, literature, and/or culture

According to the Legion of Mary, one of their members, Ven. Edel Quinn, was accidentally baptized "Edelweiss," as the hard-of-hearing priest misheard her father when asked the baby's name. It seems Ven. Edel didn't care for Edelweiss, and so shortened it to Edel, which has since been bestowed on Irish and non-Irish girls in her honor.[19] The Edel Gathering — an annual Catholic conference for women of faith — was also named for Ven. Edel Quinn.[20]

Edessa

Pronunciation: \ ə-ˈdes-sə, ē-ˈdes-sə \

Edessa was the ancient name for modern-day Urfa, in southeastern Turkey, where Christianity was introduced soon after the time of Jesus, and a Christian council was held in the late second century. A miraculous image of Our Lady, said to have alerted people to the holiness of St. Alexius of Rome (also known as St. Alexis the Beggar), is known as Our Lady of Edessa.

Nicknames: Dess, Dessa, Dessie, Eddy, Edie

Feast day: June 2 (Our Lady of Edessa)

Elizabeth

Pronunciation: \ e-ˈli-zə-bəth \

I went back and forth on whether or not to include Elizabeth in this volume, and ultimately decided that St. Elizabeth's connection with Our Lady as shown in the Visitation (Second Joyful Mystery of the Rosary) was more than enough to qualify it as a name with impeccable Marian character — especially since it is to St. Elizabeth (during the Visitation) that Our Lady proclaims her song of praise known as the *Magnificat* — as well as the fact that the name Lily, which immediately calls to mind Our Lady's flowers of the same name, is a traditional nickname for Elizabeth.

Nicknames: Bess, Beth, Bets(e)y, Betty, Eliza, Elle, Ellie, Elsa, Elsie, Libbett, Libby, Liddy, Lies(e)l, Lilibet, Lily, Lisa, Lisette, Liz, Liza, Lizzie, Sabeth, Tess (and many others)

Variants: Elisabeth (various), Elisabetta (Italian), Elise, Isabel (various), Isabella (various), Isabelle (various), Lisa (various)

Feast day: May 31 (Visitation of the Blessed Virgin Mary)

See also: Lily, Magnificat, Visitación

Eve

Pronunciation: \ ˈēv \

Eve comes from Hebrew, meaning "to breathe" or "to live." It is used in reference to Our Lady as the New Eve, the woman who was to counterbalance the sin of the first Eve (who brought sin into the world) by bringing salvation into the world (Jesus).

Nicknames: Evie, Evita

Variants: Aoife (Irish, used as a Gaelicization of Eve, though not etymologically related), Ava (English), Chava (Hebrew), Eva (various), Eveleen (English), Evita (Spanish), Ewa (Polish)

Feast day: March 25 (Annunciation)

See also: Ave

Faith

Pronunciation: \ ˈfāth \

One of Our Lady's French titles is *Notre Dame de la Foi* ("Our Lady of Faith"), and as such she is revered in several locales, including Gravelines (where the medieval faithful would leave money for the poor in a hollow tree at night), La Cauchie (where a statue of Our Lady mysteriously relocated from a chapel to the oak tree hollow where it had been discovered), and Amiens (where the Augustinian convent celebrates the miracles obtained through prayer in front of an image of Our Lady of Faith every year on April 29). There's also devotion to her in Canada under the title Our Lady of Foie.

Additionally, she's revered under the Spanish title *Santa María de Fe* ("Holy Mary of Faith"), with the corresponding given names María de Fe, Marifé (which is also used as a nickname of María de Fe), and even the trim Fe.

Variants: Fay, Faye, María de Fe, Marifé
Feast day: April 29 (Our Lady of Faith)
See also: Charity, Grace, Hope

Fatima

Pronunciation: \ˈfa-tə-mə\

This name has a long and important history in the Islamic world — Fatima was a daughter of the Prophet Muhammad, through which

all of his descendants flow. However, for Roman Catholics, Fatima has risen to prominence as the name of a very holy place — that of Fátima, Portugal, where Our Lady appeared to three shepherd children (Lucia Dos Santos and her cousins Francisco and Jacinta Marto) in 1917. I've seen the first name-middle name combinations Maria Fatima and Maria de Fatima as well, which makes the Marian aspect more obvious.

Nicknames: Fia, Fima, Tima

Feast day: May 13 (Our Lady of Fátima)

See also: Akita, Banneux (b), Beauraing (b), Francis, Francisco (b), Guadalupe, Guadalupe (b), Kibeho, Kibeho (b), Knock, Lourdes, Salette, Tepeyac (b), Walsingham (b)

Fiat

Pronunciation: \ ˈfē-ät \

Though I've never seen it used as a personal name, Fiat is distinctly Marian — it refers to Our Lady's free-will decision to bear the Savior in her womb, as God the Father asked her to through the Archangel Gabriel. "Behold, I am the handmaid of the Lord," she'd said. "May it be done to me according to your word" (Lk 1:38). *Fiat* is Latin for "let it be it done."

The middle name spot is always a good place for a rare or unusual name, and Fiat is probably best suited for that position. A friend of mine considered the first name-middle name combination Marian Fiat for her daughter, which I love.

Nicknames: Fee, Fia

Feast day: March 25 (Annunciation)

See also: Ancilla, Annunziata, Gabriel (b), Gabriela, Nunzio (b)

Fiat in real life, literature, and/or culture

Though Fiat's Marian connection is indisputable, it should also be remembered that Fiat is also the name of a well-known European car. However, I would think this would pose no more of a problem than the fact that proper names Sienna and Mercedes, for example, have corresponding vehicle names.

Gabriela

Pronunciation: \ ga-brē-ˈe-lə, gä-brē-ˈe-lə \

This feminine form of Gabriel points to the Annunciation (First Joyful Mystery of the Rosary), when the Angel Gabriel told Mary that she'd been chosen by God to conceive and bear His Son: "Behold, I am the handmaid of the Lord. May it be done to me according to your word" (Lk 1:38).

Nicknames: Bree, Bri, Briella, Brielle, Ella, Ellie, Gabby, Gabi

Variants: Briella (English), Brielle (English, French), Gabriella (various), Gabrielle (French)

Feast day: March 25 (Annunciation)

See also: Ancilla, Annunziata, Fiat, Gabriel (b), Nunzio (b)

Grace

Pronunciation: \ ˈgrās \

Grace (derived from the Latin *gratia*) "is *favor, the free and undeserved help* that God gives us to respond to his call to become children of God, adoptive sons, partakers of the divine nature and of eternal life[21] … Grace is a *participation in the life of God*" (*CCC*, 1996, 1997; emphasis as in original).

Our Lady was hailed by the Angel Gabriel at the Annunciation as being "full of grace" (Latin: *gratia plena*); these words of the Angel begin our beloved prayer: "Hail Mary, full of grace!"

She is also known by the title "Our Lady of Grace," and there is a popular and well-known image of her under this title with arms outstretched, standing on the earth with the serpent under her foot.

Nickname: Gracie

Variants: Gracia (Spanish), Graciela (Spanish), Gracja (Polish), Gráinne (Irish, anglicized as Grace), Grania/Granya (Irish, anglicized spellings of Gráinne), Gratia (Latin, German), Grazia (Italian), Graziella (Italian)

Feast day: May 31 (Our Lady of Grace)

See also: Altagracia, Charity, Faith, Gratian (b), Hope

Grace in real life, literature, and/or culture
The lovely Grace Kelly, 1950s Hollywood starlet and princess of Monaco (wife of Prince Rainier), may have started the "Grace" trend with her charmed life, and since her untimely death in 1982, its popularity has increased, with the most recent figures from the SSA (2015) revealing its use as a first name at the number 19 spot. Its use as a middle name isn't measured, but my personal experience indicates it's one of the go-to Marian middle names (like Marie in the past).

Guadalupe

Pronunciation: \ gwä-də-ˈlü-pä, ˈgwä-də-ˌlüp \

This given name is from the Spanish Marian title *Nuestra Señora de Guadalupe* ("Our Lady of Guadalupe"), referring to an apparition by Our Lady to St. Juan Diego Cuauhtlatoatzin in Guadalupe, Mexico in the 16ᵗʰ century. Though commonly used as a girl's name, Guadalupe is also used as a man's name in Spanish-speaking locales.

Nicknames: Lupe, Lupita

Feast day: December 12 (Our Lady of Guadalupe)

See also: Akita, Banneux (b), Beauraing (b), Fatima, Guadalupe (b), Juan Diego (b), Kibeho, Kibeho (b), Knock (b), Lourdes, Rose, Salette, Tepeyac (b), Tilma, Walsingham (b)

Gwenfair

Pronunciation: \ gwen-ˈvī(-ə)r (Welsh), ˈgwen-fer (English) \

This lovely Welsh name is made up of the elements *gwen*, meaning "fair, white, blessed," and Mair, the Welsh version of Mary. Though the proper Welsh pronunciation is \ gwen-ˈvī(-ə)r \ (to rhyme with "fire"), I don't think it's unreasonable to use the pronunciation \ ˈgwen-fer \ in the U.S.

Nicknames: Gwen, Gwennie

Variants: Mairwen (Welsh), Maïwenn (Breton), Mari-Gwenn (Breton)

Feast day: September 12 (Most Holy Name of Mary)

See also: Beata, Benedict (b), Benedicta, Biancamaria, Ivory, Ivory (b), Mairwen

Hailemariam

Pronunciation: \ hī-lā-ˈmer-ē-əm \

In a December 2016 BBC article on African naming traditions, I was delighted to read that Hailemariam is a name used in Ethiopia for Our Lady.[22] Although it's a masculine name in Ethopia, I think in America it would be most comfortable for a girl.

Nicknames: Hailey, Hy, Mari, Mariam, Mary

Variant: Haile-Mariam

Feast day: March 25 (Annunciation)

See also: Ave

Hailemariam in real life, literature, and/or culture
Hailemariam Desalegn is the current Prime Minister of Ethiopia, having assumed office in 2012.

Holly

Pronunciation: \ ˈhä-lē \

Christmas holly (*Ilex opaca* et al.) has been known as Saint Mary's Holly and represents the perpetual virginity of Our Lady.

Feast day : October 16 (Purity of the Blessed Virgin Mary)

See also: Pureza, Virginia

Hope

Pronunciation: \ ˈhōp \

Hope can be a virtue name, in the manner of Faith and Grace, but it can also be a Marian name, for her title Our Lady of Hope, also known as Our Lady of Hope of Pontmain and Our Lady of Pontmain, for an apparition of Our Lady that occurred at Pontmain, France, in 1871, during the Franco-Prussian War, after the villagers prayed for protection. During this apparition, Our Lady referred to herself as the "Madonna of the Crucifix."[23]

Variants: Espérance (French), Esperanza (Spanish), Nadia (various), Nadine (French), Sperantia (Latin)

Feast day: January 17 (Our Lady of Hope, also known as Our Lady of Pontmain)

See also: Charity, Cruz, Cruz (b), Faith, Grace, Madonna

Ianua

Pronunciation: \ ē-ˈä-nü-ə, ˈyä- nü-ə, ˈyä-nwä \

In the Litany of Loreto, Our Lady is referred to in Latin as *Ianua Caeli* — "Gate of Heaven."

Nickname: Iana

Variant: Janua (Our Lady's title "Gate of Heaven" is sometimes written *Janua Coeli*, pronounced the same as *Ianua Caeli*)

Feast day: September 12 (Most Holy Name of Mary)

See also: Araceli, Caeli, Celeste, Celestine (b)

***Ianua* in real life, literature, and/or culture**
I'd never seen nor heard of this word being used as a name until one of my readers shared with me the name of her niece, Ianua Caeli, after Our Lady, Gate of Heaven. How unusual and lovely!

Iciar

Pronunciation: \ ē-ˈsē-är, ˈē-sē-är \

Iciar appears to be the most common spelling of this name, coming from the name Itziar, which is the name of a small town in the Pyrenees on the Way of St. James (*Camino de Santiago*). It's a Basque name, possibly meaning "old stone," "high point facing the sea," or "sight from the top of the peak." The 17th-century church there is dedicated to the Virgin of Itziar, and it's believed to be on the site of an earlier church dating to the 13th century.

The story of Our Lady of Itziar seems similar to that of Our Lady of Aránzazu (see Ainhoa, Aranza) — tradition holds that a girl found the Blessed Virgin between black thorns (it is unclear whether this means a statue of the Blessed Virgin, or an apparition of Our Lady herself), and understood that Our Lady wanted a church built in that spot. However, the ground was steep and difficult to build upon, so construction was planned for a different, flatter site. At night, the stones moved mysteriously to the site of the discovery of the Blessed Virgin, and so the difficult terrain was dealt with and the church was built where Our Lady requested. The original building has since been replaced by a newer one, dating to the 16th century. There is a statue there, revered as Our Lady of Itziar, thought to have been carved in the 13th century. She is the patroness of seafarers.

Nicknames: Ici, Icie

Variants: Itxiar, Itziar, Iziar

Feast Day: First Sunday in August (Our Lady of Itziar)

See also: Ainhoa, Aranza, Hawthorn (b)

Idoia

Pronunciation: \ ē-ˈdȯi-a \

From the word *idoia*, possibly meaning "pond," "pit," or "well" in Basque, this refers to Our Lady of Idoia — a statue of Our Lady with the Infant Jesus seated on her knee, in which both are smiling. Tradition holds that the statue was found in a pond or similar in the town of Isaba in Navarre, Spain, in the late 13th or early 14th century.

Nickname: Idie

Variant: Idoya

Feast day: Whit Monday (the day after Pentecost)
(Our Lady of Idoia)

Idoia in real life, literature, and/or culture
On the first Sunday in July, the Feast of Idoias is held in Spain, in which women named Idoia gather at the chapel of the Virgin of Idoia to celebrate.

Immaculata

Pronunciation: \ i-ma-kyü-ˈlä-tä \

From the Latin for "pure, without stain," *Immaculata* is used in honor of the Immaculate Conception of Mary. This Catholic doctrine holds that Our Lady was conceived without the stain of original sin — that

she was immaculately conceived. This doctrine was promulgated in the apostolic letter *Ineffabilis Deus* (*Ineffable God*) on December 8, 1854, by Pope Pius IX.

Nicknames: Imma, Immie, Lata, Lottie, Mac, Max

Variants: Immacolata (Italian), Immaculée (French), Inmaculada (Spanish)

Feast Day: December 8 (Immaculate Conception)

See also: Beauraing (b), Concepción, Ivory, Ivory (b), Kolbe (b), Lourdes, Maximilian (b), Pureza

Immaculata, Immaculée in real life, literature, and/or culture
Though Immaculata may be somewhat familiar as part of a nun or sister's name (e.g., Sr. Mary Immaculata), I'd never heard of the name used for a child until I met one of my dear friends whose daughter is named Faith Immaculata. I was immediately struck by its significance, and felt inspired to look up other somewhat unusual or seldom-used Marian names, and to compile my findings into this book. Thank you to my little friend Faith Immaculata and her parents who named her so well!

Immaculée Ilibagiza is a famous bearer of this variant, having survived the 1994 Rwandan genocide and become an author and motivational speaker.

Incoronata

Pronunciation: \ in-kȯr-ə-ˈnä-tä \

This beautiful name, meaning "crowned," refers to two separate Marian associations: the first is the discovery of a miraculous image of the Crowned Virgin in Foggia, Italy in April of the year 1001; the second is the Crowning (Coronation) of the Virgin Mary as Queen of Heaven (Fifth Glorious Mystery of the Rosary).

Nicknames: Cora, Corona

Variants: Coronada (Spanish), Coronata (Italian)

Feast day: August 22 (Queenship of Mary)

See also: Aurea, Caeli, Candace, Corona, Marigold, Regina, Reginald (b), Reina

Incoronata in real life, literature, and/or culture
As with the previous entry (Immaculata), I first heard Incoronata as the middle name of the daughter of a friend. It was given in tribute of her Italian grandmother, who had the same middle name; no doubt her grandmother was given the name with Our Lady in mind.

Iris

Pronunciation: \ ˈī-rəs \

Two different species of iris flowers have beautiful connections to Our Lady. *Iris florentina* has also been known as the Madonna Iris and represents Our Lady's lineage from the house of King David and her status as Queen; *Iris germanica*, or the German bearded iris, has been called Mary's Sword of Sorrow, as its leaves resemble swords.

Feast day: September 15 (Our Lady of Sorrows)

See also: Addolorata, David (b), Dolores, Ivy, Piedad, Pierce (b), Pieta, Simeon (b), Tristan (b)

Isla

Pronunciation: \ ˈī-lə (Scottish), ˈēs-la (Spanish) \

Isla is a Scottish given name, after the Scottish Hebrides island Islay (which can also be pronounced \ ˈī-lə \), and it can also be a Spanish name, as *isla* is the Spanish word for "island." In both cases, its Marian character comes from the title "Our Lady of the Isles" (*Moire ro Naomh nan Eilean* in Scottish Gaelic, referring to a statue of Our Lady on the island of South Uist in the Outer Hebrides of Scotland), or any of the devotions in the U.S. and Canada to Our Lady of the Island or Our Lady of the Isle, including churches and institutions in New York, Rhode Island, Massachusetts, and Quebec, Canada. There's also the church of Our Lady of the Isle in Croatia.

Variant: Islay (Scottish)

Feast day: August 15 (Assumption; the Scottish statue of Our Lady of the Isles was dedicated on this day in 1958)

Isla in real life, literature, and/or culture
Isla is perhaps most familiar to Americans due to Australian actress Isla Fisher. Though I couldn't find anyone famous with the \ ˈēs-la \ pronunciation, there were several comments by readers on various name sites who have the name Isla and use the Spanish pronunciation.

Ivory

Pronunciation: \ ˈīv-rē, ˈī-və-rē \

"Tower of Ivory" (_Turris eburnea_) is one of the titles of Our Lady included in the Litany of Loreto. According to the SSA, the name Ivory has regularly been among the top 1,000 names for both boys and girls in the U.S. since 1900.

Nicknames: Ivie, Ivy

Feast days: October 16 (Purity of the Blessed Virgin Mary)
December 8 (Immaculate Conception)

See also: Biancamaria, Gwenfair, Immaculata, Ivory (b), Mairwen, Pureza

Ivy

Pronunciation: \ ˈī-vē \

Kenilworth ivy (*Cymbalaria muralis*) has also been known as Tears of Mary.

Feast day: September 15 (Our Lady of Sorrows)

See also: Addolorata, Angustias, Dolores, Iris, Piedad, Pierce (b), Pieta, Simeon (b), Tristan (b)

Juniper

Pronunciation: \ ˈjü-nə-pər \

The juniper tree (*Juniperis*) has been known as the Madonna's Juniper Bush because, according to pious tradition, it sheltered the Holy Family during their flight into Egypt, thus hiding them and protecting them from Herod's men.

Nicknames: June, Junie, Juno

Feast day: January 1 (Mary, Mother of God)

See also: Juniper (b), Madonna, Rosemary

Kibeho

Pronunciation: \ ki-ˈbā-hō \

Our Lady appeared to several teenagers in the town of Kibeho in Rwanda, Africa from 1981-1989 with a message of repentance, fasting, and praying the Rosary, and foretold what many believe to be the Rwandan genocide of 1994. Immaculée Ilibagiza is a famous survivor of the genocide, who spreads awareness of Our Lady of Kibeho through her writing and speaking.

Nicknames: Bay, Kay, Kib, Kibbie

Feast day: November 28 (Our Lady of Kibeho)

See also: Akita, Amabilis (b), Banneux (b), Beauraing (b), Fatima, Guadalupe, Guadalupe (b), Immaculata, Kibeho (b), Knock (b), Lourdes, Salette, Tepeyac (b), Walsingham (b)

Laetitia

Pronunciation: \ lə-ˈtish-ə, le-ˈtē-syä, lī-ˈtē-tē-ä \

Laetitia is Latin for "joy, happiness," and is part of the Marian title *Causa Nostrae Laetitiae* (Cause of Our Joy).

Nicknames: Lecia, Leti, Lettie, Letty, Tisha

Variants: Latisha (English), Leticia (Spanish), Letitia (English), Letizia (Italian), Lettice (English)

Feast day: December 2 (Our Lady of Joy, also known as Our Lady of Liesse)

See also: Beatrix, Leeson (b), Liesse, Maeve

Lavender

Pronunciation: \ ˈla-vən-dər \

The lavender plant (*Lavandula officinalis*) has been known as Mary's Drying Plant, as tradition holds that Our Lady dried her Little Boy's clothes on a lavender bush, and the scent of His skin transferred to the flowers.

Nicknames: Lav, Lavvy

Feast day: January 1 (Mary, Mother of God)

Letteria

Pronunciation: \ lə-'ter-ē-ä \

The story of *Madonna della Lettera* (Our Lady of the Letter) is a fascinating one. Tradition holds that St. Paul came to Messina, Italy to evangelize, and some of the people wanted to return to the Holy Land with him in order to meet Our Lady. One of them did, bearing a letter from the people of Messina, and Our Lady wrote back, tying the rolled letter with a strand of her hair, which is still kept in the Cathedral of Messina. The name Letteria is bestowed on girls in honor of Our Lady of the Letter, and is traditionally nicknamed Lilla.

Nicknames: Letty, Lilla, Teria
Feast day: June 3 (Our Lady of the Letter)

Liesse

Pronunciation: \ lē-'es \

Our Lady of Liesse (*Notre Dame de Liesse*) means "Our Lady of Joy," and is revered in the town of Liesse-Notre-Dame in northern France, whose basilica has been a pilgrimage destination since the 12th century. The original statue of Our Lady of Liesse — one of the Black Madonnas — is said to have been brought to France by three Crusaders who had been captured by Saracens and refused to convert to Islam. It was destroyed during the French Revolution, but a copy stands in its place, and Our Lady of Liesse continues to be revered.

Nicknames: Lee, Essie

Feast day: December 2 (Our Lady of Liesse)

See also: Beatrix, Laetitia, Leeson (b), Maeve

Liesse in real life, literature, and/or culture
A quick Google search reveals quite a few women — including a
religious sister — with the name Marie-Liesse (mostly in France).
How beautiful!

Lily

Pronunciation: \ ˈli-lē \

Lilies are rife with Marian associations — St. Bede likened the petals
of the white lily to Our Lady's purity and its golden anthers to the
glorious nature of her soul, and they are often used in art to symbol-
ize her purity (e.g., St. Gabriel the Archangel is traditionally depicted
holding a lily in his hand during the Annunciation).

Our Lady of the Lily is a title venerated in Spain, after an image of
the Madonna and Child was said to have miraculously come from a
lily. The lily of the valley (_Convallaria majalis_) has been called Mary's
Tears, and Mary is also understood to be the "lily of the valleys" from
the Song of Songs (2:1).

Lily is also a traditional nickname for Elizabeth.

Variants: Líle (Irish), Lili (various), Lilia, Lilian, Liliana, Lilias (Scottish), Lillian, Lillianne, Lillie, Lilly, Lilli (various), Lilya (various), Liliya (various)

Feast days: March 25 (Annunciation)
October 16 (Purity of the Blessed Virgin Mary)

See also: Annunziata, Concepción, Elizabeth, Immaculata, Maylis, Pureza, Susanna

Lola

Pronunciation: \ ˈlō-lə \

This beautiful name warrants its own entry because I think it's a current, fashionable name whose Marian attributes should be made known. Lola is a traditional nickname for Dolores, a name that refers to Our Lady of Sorrows (*Nuestra Señora de los Dolores*), and, while I think it can stand on its own, it can also serve as a nickname for a host of other names like Addolorata, Lourdes, and Violet.

Feast day: September 15 (Our Lady of Sorrows)
See also: Addolorata, Dolores, Lourdes, Violet

Lola in real life, literature, and/or culture
In the past, I think Lola might have been a concern to parents who didn't care for the name's pop culture associations, such as the song "Lola" by The Kinks and "Copacabana" by Barry Manilow, and the 1961 movie "Lola," never mind the name's diminutive, Lolita (see Dolores). But more recently, I've seen parents really loving the name Lola — both as a given name and as a nickname for

beautiful names related to our faith, such as Lourdes — and it seems that any past negative associations with this name are becoming ancient history.

Loretta

Pronunciation: \ lə-ˈre- tə \

Loretta has traditionally been used as a variant of Loreto, which is the name of a small town in Italy where stands a small house, held by tradition to be the house in which Our Lady was born and grew up, and in which the Annunciation and the Incarnation took place (known as the Holy House of Nazareth). Angels are said to have carried the house there in the 13th century. The Litany of Loreto (*Litaniae Lauretanae* in Latin), also known as the Litany of the Blessed Virgin Mary, lists many of Our Lady's beautiful titles.

Nicknames: Etty, Lora, Lori, Rett, Retta

Variants: Loreta (Italian), Loreto (Italian, Spanish), Lorita (Italian)

Feast days: March 6 (Our Lady of Nazareth)
March 25 (Annunciation)

See also: Annunziata, Loreto (b), Nazaret, Nazario (b), Nunzio (b)

Loretta in real life, literature, and/or culture
My grandmother's given name was Mary Loretta, though she mostly went by Loretta, and sometimes by Rett. She was of Irish descent,

and thus a good example of the usability of this name by non-Italians.

Lourdes

Pronunciation: \ ˈlȯrdz, ˈlu̇rdz, ˈlu̇r-dās (Spanish) \

Lourdes is the name of the town in France where St. Bernadette Soubirous received visions of Our Lady in 1858. One of the many remarkable things about the visions was that Our Lady told Bernadette that she was "the Immaculate Conception" — a doctrine that had been officially proclaimed by the Church only four years previously. Since then, Lourdes has been a place of pilgrimage and miracles.

Nicknames: Lola, Lou, Lula, Lulu

Variant: Lurdes (Spanish)

Feast Day: February 11 (Our Lady of Lourdes)

See also: Akita, Banneux (b), Beauraing (b), Concepción, Fatima, Guadalupe, Guadalupe (b), Immaculata, Kibeho, Kibeho (b), Knock (b), Salette, Tepeyac (b), Walsingham (b)

Lourdes in real life, literature, and/or culture

Über entertainer Madonna named her daughter as she herself was named, drawing from her Catholic roots for a Marian name when selecting the name Lourdes (who often goes by the equally Marian "Lola"). I've seen Lourdes used or strongly considered by Catholic

families who love this Marian place name with traditional usage as a first name (alone or paired with a form of Mary, which sometimes renders the nickname Mary Lou).

Lux, Luz

Pronunciation: \ ˈləks (Lux), ˈlüs (Luz: Spanish — Latin America), ˈlüth (Luz: Spanish — Spain) \

Lux and *luz* mean "light" in Latin and Spanish, respectively. Lux Veritatis (*Light of the Truth*) is the name of the 1931 Pope Pius XI encyclical that celebrated the 1,500[th] anniversary of the Council of Ephesus, during which Mary's title as Mother of God was declared. Luz comes from the Spanish Marian title *Nuestra Señora de la Luz* ("Our Lady of Light"), an image of which is in the cathedral of León in León, Mexico.

Nicknames: Lou, Lu, Lucy, Lulu

Variants: Luce (French, Italian), Lucette (French), Lucia (various), Luciana (various), Lucie (French), Lucilla (Italian), Lucille (French), Lucinda (English, Portuguese), Lucy (English)

Feast Day: February 27 (Our Lady of Light)

See also: Lucian (b), Madonna, Theotokos (b)

Macarena

Pronunciation: \ ma-kə-ˈrā-nə \

La Macarena is the name of a district in the city of Seville, Spain, where is found the Basilica of Our Lady of Hope of Macarena (*Nuestra Señora de la Esperanza de Macarena*), who herself is also referred to as *La Macarena*. The title refers to a 17th-century wooden statue of Our Lady, portrayed weeping with glass tears, who is the center of a 400-year-old Good Friday tradition: a 12-hour procession attended by pilgrims from all over the world.

Nicknames: Cara, Mac, Rena

Feast day: December 18 (Our Lady of Hope of Macarena)

Macarena in real life, literature, and/or culture
I think most people these days are familiar with the name Macarena because of the Spanish dance song by the same name, which does, in fact, refer to a girl with the traditional Marian name Macarena.

Madonna

Pronunciation: \ mə-ˈdä-nə \

Madonna means "my lady" in Italian. It has long been used to refer to Our Lady, and has long been bestowed on girls in her honor. Additionally, "Madonna" is a term employed by art historians to refer to depictions of Our Lady from the Italian Renaissance, and the term "Madonna and Child" is familiar to many.

Nicknames: Maddy, Donna
Feast day: January 1 (Mary, Mother of God)
See also: Candace, Despina, Mitrofan (b), Theotokos (b)

Madonna in real life, literature, and/or culture
Though Madonna is a gorgeous, impeccably Marian name with a long history of use for Catholic girls, entertainer Madonna (born Madonna Louise Ciccone) has unfortunately become one of the people most closely associated with the name, and has rendered it unusable for most Catholic families. Happily, I'm seeing the tide turning a bit: I interviewed Hope Schneir from the band "Hope and Justin" on my blog,[24] and she shared that one of her daughters is named Indigo Madonna (named specifically for Our Lady); I know another set of parents who were also considering the name Madonna as a middle name for their baby girl. I think the middle name is a perfect spot for it, and a good way to ease the name back into use by the faithful.

Mae, May

Pronunciation: \ ˈmā \

May is a traditional diminutive of Mary, and also points to the month of May, which has traditionally been devoted to Our Lady. The variant Mae also has traditional usage.

Feast day: September 12 (Most Holy Name of Mary)

Maeve

Pronunciation: \ ˈmāv \

This beautiful Irish name has become more and more popular since it first entered the top 1,000 names for girls in the U.S. twenty years ago. I've seen people bestow it on their daughters in honor of Our Lady, mistakenly considering it to be a variant of Mary, but I do believe it can be considered Marian in a different way: the *Baby Names of Ireland* website, which recorded the late Irish author Frank McCourt saying each name the way it would be pronounced in Ireland, presents one of the meanings of Maeve as "cause of great joy," which is similar to Our Lady's title "Cause of Our Joy" (*Causa Nostrae Laetitiae*).[25] Additionally, it would not be out of bounds for parents to combine the names Mary and Eve into Maeve.

Nicknames: Mae, Maevey

Variants: Madb, Maebh, Mave, Méabh, Meadhbh, Medb

Feast day: December 2 (Our Lady of Joy, also known as Our Lady of Liesse)

See also: Beatrix, Laetitia, Leeson (b), Liesse

Magnificat

Pronunciation: \ mag-ˈni-fi-kät \

In the *Liturgy of the Hours* (the "daily prayer of the Church," involving five times of prayer throughout the day), Evening Prayer includes the "Canticle of Mary," also known as the *Magnificat*, after the first word of the first line in Latin: *Magnificat anima mea Dominum* ("My soul proclaims the greatness of the Lord"). It's the beautiful prayer of blessing and adoration that Our Lady exclaims after hearing Elizabeth's greeting during the Visitation (Second Joyful Mystery of the Rosary). Though I've never seen Magnificat used as a given name, its similarity in sound and nickname possibility to Magdalene and Margaret makes it quite feasible.

Nickname: Maggie

Feast day: May 31 (Visitation of the Blessed Virgin Mary)

See also: Elizabeth, Fiat, Visitación

Mairwen

Pronunciation: \ ˈmī(-ə)r-wen (Welsh), ˈmer-wen (English) \

This lovely Welsh name is a combination of the elements Mair, which is Welsh for "Mary," and *wen*, which means "white, fair, blessed." Though the authentic Welsh pronunciation is \ ˈmī(-ə)r-wen \, I think it would be reasonable to use \ ˈmer-wen \ in the U.S.

Nicknames: Mair, Mari, Mary

Variants: Gwenfair (Welsh), Maïwenn (Breton), Mari-Gwenn (Breton)

Feast day: September 12 (Most Holy Name of Mary)

See also: Beata, Benedict (b), Benedicta, Biancamaria, Gwenfair, Ivory, Ivory (b)

Maite

Pronunciation: \ ˈmī-tā \

Maite is a Spanish name — a contraction of Maria and Teresa — and a pretty twist on the compound Marian names like Maryanne, Marilee, etc.

Variant: Mayte

Feast day: September 12 (Most Holy Name of Mary)

See also: Marisa

Maria, Marie

See Mary.

Mariae

Pronunciation: \ ˈmär-ē-ā \

Mariae is the Latin genitive form of Mary, meaning "belonging to Mary" (e.g., the name of the papal encyclical *Rosarium Virginis Mariae* [*The Rosary of the Virgin Mary*], in which the Luminous Mysteries of the Rosary were revealed). What an extra meaningful Marian name!

Nicknames: Mae, Mari

Feast day: September 12 (Most Holy Name of Mary)

See also: Demaris

Mariales, Marialis

Pronunciation: \ mer-ē-ˈä-lās (Mariales), mer-ē-ˈä-lis (Marialis), mä-rē-ə-ˈlēs (Marialis) \

In his book *Champions of the Rosary*, Fr. Calloway quoted a bit from John S. Johnson's *The Rosary in Action*, which included the word *Mariales*, referring to Marian books.[26] I loved that! It reminded me of the title of Pope Paul VI's 1974 apostolic exhortation *Marialis Cultus* (*Marian Devotion*), and both Mariales and Marialis seemed eminently doable to me as given names. Marialis also seems like it could be considered a combination of Maria and Lis (which could be short for Elisabeth, or could refer to lilies, à la fleur-de-lis).

Nicknames: Lis, Lisa, Mari, Maria, Molly

Feast day: September 12 (Most Holy Name of Mary)

See also: Elizabeth, Lily

Mariamante

Pronunciation: \ mä-rē-ä-ˈmän-tā \

Combining the elements Maria (for Our Lady, of course) and *amante* (Latin for "lover"), Mariamante literally translates as "Lover of Mary," a beautiful name for anyone wanting to demonstrate their devotion to Our Lady.

Nicknames: Mante, Maria, Mia

Feast day: September 12 (Most Holy Name of Mary)

Mariamante in real life, literature, and/or culture

The Apostolate of Holy Motherhood is a small book detailing the purported visions of Our Lady to a young mother in Ohio from February through August of 1987. The young mother, in order to preserve her anonymity, published the book under the name Mariamante.

Marianella

Pronunciation: \ mä-rē-ən-ˈel-la \

Marianella is a gorgeous place name — in fact, the place near Naples where St. Alphonsus Liguori was born.

Nicknames: Mari, Maria, Mary, Nell, Nella

Feast day: September 12 (Most Holy Name of Mary)

See also: Alphonsus (b)

Mariazell

Pronunciation: \ mä-rē-ät-ˈzel, mä-rē-ä-ˈzel \

Mariazell is the name of a town in Austria, deriving its name from a miraculous occurrence with a statue of Our Lady: In the 12th century, a monk named Magnus was sent from the Benedictine Monastery of St. Lambrecht to minister to the people of the area in which Mariazell currently stands. When a rock blocked his way, he implored Our Lady for help, and the rock split. When he reached his destination, he built a "cell" for himself and the statue, which also served as a chapel. *Mariazell* means "Mary in the cell," and the Basilica of Mariazell (also known as *Basilica Mariä Geburt* ["Basilica of the Birth of the Virgin Mary"]), still houses the statue, which is referred to as *Magnus Mater Austriae* ("Great Mother of Austria").

Nicknames: Mari, Maria, Mary, Mazie, Mia, Zell, Zellie

Variant: Mariatzell

Feast day: September 13 (Our Lady of Mariazell)

Mariazell in real life, literature, and/or culture

I first heard of Mariazell from one of the readers of my blog, who wrote: "It is a very meaningful place to the [Franciscan University of Steubenville] students who have studied abroad in Gaming, Austria.

I could see it being a very pretty name for a little girl — Mariazell. It also could be seen as a mash-up of St. Zelie Martin's full name, Marie-Azélie. Could go by nicknames: Zell, Zelie, Mia, Mari, Mazie."[27]

Marigold

Pronunciation: \ ˈmer-ə-gōld, ˈmär-ə-gōld \

The marigold flower (*Calendula officinalis*) was named after Our Lady, combining her name with the word "gold" — "Mary's gold."

Nicknames: Goldie, Maggie, Margie, Margo, Mari, Mary

Variant: Marygold

Feast day: August 22 (Queenship of Mary)

See also: Aurea, Candace, Corona, Incoronata, Regina, Reginald (b), Reina

Marigold in real life, literature, and/or culture

Fans of "Downton Abbey" will remember that Edith's daughter was named Marigold, and *Lord of the Rings* enthusiasts may be aware that character Samwise Gamgee's youngest sister was Marigold. (His other sisters were the equally Marian Daisy and May!) In real life, I know of several little girls named Marigold (first name or middle), and one of their mothers told me the appellation was specifically in honor of the Crowned Mary.

Marina

Pronunciation: \ mə-ˈrē-nə \

Marina can be connected to Our Lady in two different ways: first, it means "of the sea," and so can be a nod to Our Lady's title "Star of the Sea" (*Stella Maris*). Second, it has usage in Scotland as an anglicization of the Scottish form of Mary, Màiri.

Nicknames: Mari, Mina, Rina

Variants: Maren (Norwegian, Danish), Marijn (Dutch),
Marine (French), Marinella (Italian),
Marinka (Croatian, Slovene), Marna (Danish)

Feast day: September 27 (Our Lady, Star of the Sea)

See also: Demaris, Maris, Stella

Maris

Pronunciation: \ ˈmer-is \

Meaning "of the sea" in Latin, Maris comes from the Marian title *Stella Maris* ("Star of the Sea").

Variants: Maristela (Portuguese, Spanish), Maristella (Italian)

Feast day: September 27 (Our Lady, Star of the Sea)

See also: Demaris, Marina, Stella

Maris in real life, literature, and/or culture
Though the association of the name Maris with an unlikable TV character is a strong one for many, it won't always be so — and using the name is one of the most effective ways to hasten its reclamation!

Marisa

Pronunciation: \ mə-ˈri-sə (English), mə-ˈrē-zə (Italian), mə-ˈrē-sə (Spanish) \

The lovely "Marisa" is a curious name — some sources give it as a contraction of names like Maria and Luisa, Maria and Isabel, and Maria and Teresa, while others say it's an elaboration of Mary, Maria, or Maris. Either way, it's impeccably Marian.

Nicknames: Mari, Mia, Misa, Ree, Risa

Variant: Marissa

Feast day: September 12 (Most Holy Name of Mary)

See also: Maite, Maris

Mary

Pronunciation: \ ˈmer-ē, ˈma-rē, ˈmā-rē \

This book wouldn't be complete without an entry for Mary herself! Mary (English), Maria (various), and Marie (French) are all forms of Miryam, the name of the mother of Jesus — the mother of God. The meaning of the name is highly debated: Various sources will give "sea of bitterness," "wished-for child," and "rebelliousness" as likely meanings. My favorite explanation, given by Behind the Name and mentioned as possible by *The Catholic Encyclopedia*, is that Mary derives from the Egyptian words for "beloved."[28] Whatever its etymological meaning, however, it's the woman herself who imbues the name with holiness and sweetness, causing St. Alphonsus Liguori to exclaim, "Ah Mary! Mary most amiable! what comfort, what sweetness, what confidence, what tenderness does my soul feel only in pronouncing thy name, only in thinking of thee! I thank my God and my Lord that he has given thee, for my good, this name so sweet, so lovely, so powerful" and St. Anselm to say, "Oh name of the mother of God, thou art my love."[29]

The name of Mary has more nicknames and variants than any other name I've come across. I've attempted to include as many here as possible, while creating separate entries for a few names that I don't want to get lost in the crowd. Additionally, a special mention should be given to the many names formed by adding Mary to another name or word — some I've included as their own entries (e.g., Gwenfair, Mairwen, Maite, Marigold, Rosemary); some I've included in the "Other ideas for naming after Our Lady" section at the end of the book; and there are many, many more that already exist or that can be created.

Nicknames for and variants of Mary *(the English form of the name)*: Mae, Maidie, Mamie, Maree, Mari, Marian, Mariel, Mariot, May, Mimi, Molly, Mollie, Polly, Pollie

Nicknames for and variants of Maria *(Latin, Italian, Spanish)*:
Mariah, Mariela, Mariella, Marietta, Marilla, Maritza, Marya, Mia, Ria

Nicknames for and variants of Marie *(French)*: Manon, Marielle, Marienne, Mariette, Marion, Marise

Nicknames and variants in other languages:

• *Basque:* Maia, Miren • *Dutch:* Maaike, Marieke, Mariette, Marijke, Marike, Mariska, Marita, Mia, Mieke, Miep, Mies, Ria • *German:* Mareike, Marita, Meike, Mitzi • *Hawaiian:* Malia • *Hebrew:* Mariam, Mariamne, Maryam, Miriam, Miryam, Myriam (nicknames: Mimi, Mim) • *Hungarian:* Mara, Mari, Maria, Marica, Marika, Mariska • *Irish:* Máire, Mairhín, Màiri, Máirín (Mairenn), Maura, Maureen, Maurene, Maurine, Moira, Molly, Mollie, Moreen, Moya, Moyra • *Jèrrais:* Mathie, Méraïyeu (nicknames: Mathotte, Micotte, Merrotte) • *Russian:* Marya, Masha • *Scottish:* Máili, Màiri, Moirean • *Slavic and Scandinavian:* Maja, Mara, Mari, Marri *Welsh:* Mair

Feast day: September 12 (Most Holy Name of Mary)

Matrona

Pronunciation: \ mä-ˈtrō-nə \

Matrona is said to be Late Latin for "lady," and can therefore point directly to Our Lady as do *Madonna* ("my lady" in Italian) and *Despina* ("lady" in Greek).

Nicknames: Mattie, Mona, Motya (Russian), Rona, Trona

Variant: Matryona (Russian)

Feast day: September 12 (Most Holy Name of Mary)

See also: Despina, Madonna

Maylis

Pronunciation: \ mā-ˈlēs, mā-ˈlis, ˈmā-lis \

Though the etymology of Maylis — the name of a town in the south of France — is debated, most sources I consulted agreed that it's a combination of Mary and lily, especially via the French phrase *Marie à la fleur de lys* ("Mary of the Lily").

Nicknames: Mae, Lisa, Lissa

Variants: Maëlys, Mailys

Feast day: September 12 (Most Holy Name of Mary)

See also: Lily

Meike

Pronunciation: \ ˈmī-kə \

This name is one of my all-time favorite finds. I've seen the boy's name Micah used with some frequency for girls in the past few years, and finding an actual girl's name — and a Marian name at that! — that has the same sound as Micah is thrilling. Meike is a German and Dutch diminutive of Maria.

Variants: Maaike (Dutch), Mieke (Dutch)

Feast day: September 12 (Most Holy Name of Mary)

Mercedes

Pronunciation: \ mər-ˈsā-dēz (English), mər-ˈsā-dās (Spanish — Latin America), mər-ˈthā-dās (Spanish — Spain) \

Mercedes is a gorgeous, traditional Spanish girl's name meaning "mercies," derived from the Spanish title *Nuestra Señora de las Mercedes* ("Our Lady of Mercies").

Nicknames: Cede, Cedy, Merche, Mercy, Sadie

Variants: Mercè (Catalan), Merced (Spanish), Mercia, Mercy, Misericordia (Latin)

Feast day: September 24 (Our Lady of Mercy or Mercies, also known as Our Lady of Ransom)

See also: Clement (b), Clementine, Mercer (b), Mercy, Misericordia, Ransom (b)

Mercedes in real life, literature, and/or culture

Many worry that Mercedes is too tied to the luxury car brand of the same name (though it's interesting to note it was named for the daughter of the businessman who pitched the idea of this sports car to the company that ended up manufacturing and distributing it), but another association (and perhaps the ultimate inspiration behind that businessman naming his daughter Mercedes) is that of the main female character in Alexandre Dumas' *The Count of Monte Cristo*.[30]

Mercy

Pronunciation: \ ˈmər-sē \

In the 13th century, Our Lady appeared separately to St. Peter Nolasco and King James I of Aragon, asking them to start an order devoted to rescuing Christians who had been captured by Muslims. St. Peter Nolasco's confessor, the Dominican St. Raymond of Peñafort, encouraged him and King James offered his protection, and so St. Peter started the Order of Our Lady of Ransom, now called the Order of the Blessed Virgin Mary of Mercy, or the Order of Mercy, or the Mercedarians. They brought an image of Our Lady of Mercy to Lima, Peru, where it resides in the Basilica of Our Lady of Mercy.

Additionally, Our Lady of Mercy (also known as the *Madonna della Misericordia*) is associated with images of the faithful taking refuge under her cloak, also known as her veil or mantle.

Variants: Mercè (Catalan), Merced (Spanish), Mercedes (Spanish), Mercia, Misericordia (Latin)

Feast day: September 24 (Our Lady of Mercy or Mercies, also known as Our Lady of Ransom)

See also: Clement (b), Clementine, Mantle (b), Mercedes, Mercer (b), Misericordia, Ransom (b), Veil

Meritxell

Pronunciation: \ mər-ē-ˈchel \

Meritxell is a Catalan name, bestowed upon girls in honor of *Mare de Déu de Meritxell* ("Our Lady of Meritxell"). Meritxell is the name of a

village in Andorra, Spain, where in the 12th century, on three different days, a statue of Our Lady with the Baby Jesus was discovered beneath a wild rose growing out of season on the route the villagers took on their way to Mass. On the third day, the villagers also discovered a large bit of ground untouched by snow — the exact size for a chapel, which they built there and in which they kept the statue. Though the original statue and chapel were destroyed in a 1972 fire, a new chapel and a replica of the statue have taken their place.

Nicknames: Chel, Meri, Merit

Feast day: September 8 (Our Lady of Meritxell)

See also: Biancamaria, Nieves, Rose

Meryt

Pronunciation: \ ˈmer-ət \

Although the experts seem to disagree over the meaning of the name Mary, one possibility is that it comes from the Egyptian *Mery, Meryt*, meaning "cherished" or "beloved."[31]

Feast day: September 12 (Most Holy Name of Mary)

See also: Amata, Amabilis (b), Annabel, Morna

Mia

Pronunciation: \ ˈmē-ə, ˈmī-ə \

Mia is a Scandinavian, Dutch, and German diminutive of Maria, thus making this chart-topper a fully Marian name. Though I believe the

more common pronunciation to be \ ˈmē-ə \, which corresponds to the \ mə-ˈrē-ə \ pronunciation of Maria, there are some who choose to say \ ˈmī-ə \, which can correspond with the old English pronunciation of Maria: \ mə-ˈrī-ə \.

Feast day: September 12 (Most Holy Name of Mary)

Mia in real life, literature, and/or culture

Though Mia has been a top ten name in the U.S. since 2009, it didn't enter the top 1,000 until 1964, when it did so with a bang, appearing at no. 568 its first year and no. 266 the next, surely due to the fact that actress Mia Farrow achieved fame in 1964 with the TV show "Peyton Place." Perhaps less well known is that she was specifically named for Our Lady, having the gorgeous given name Maria de Lourdes.

Milagros

Pronunciation: \ mē-ˈlä-grōs \

This traditional Spanish girl's name means "miracles" and derives from the Marian title *Nuestra Señora de los Milagros* ("Our Lady of Miracles"); *milagros* is also a term for small charms that represent miracles that the bearer hopes Our Lady will assist with, or that have already happened for which the bearer is grateful.

A similar title for Our Lady is *Nuestra Señora de la Medalla Milagrosa* (Our Lady of the Miraculous Medal).

Nickname: Mila

Feast days: March 12 (Our Lady of Miracles,
St. Maur des Fossés, France)
May 6 (Our Lady of Miracles, Rome)
May 23 (Our Lady of Miracles, Brescia)
July 4 (Our Lady of Miracles, Avignon)
June 21 (Our Lady of Miracles, Alcamo, Sicily)

Miren

Pronunciation: \ ˈmid-din, ˈmē-din \

Miren is the Basque form of Maria, and has such a beautiful and unexpected pronunciation.

Feast day: September 12 (Most Holy Name of Mary)

Misericordia

Pronunciation: \ mə-ˈzer-ə-ˌkȯrd-ē-ə, mə-ˈser-ə-ˌkȯrd-ē-ə \

Latin for "mercy, compassion," Misericordia refers to *Mater Misericordiae* ("Mother of Mercy"), one of the titles for Our Lady included in the *Salve Regina*.

Nicknames: Cora, Cordy, Mia, Misa, Sera

Variants: Mercy, Merced (Spanish), Mercedes (Spanish)

Feast day: September 24 (Our Lady of Mercy or Mercies, also
known as Our Lady of Ransom)

See also: Clement (b), Clementine, Mercer (b), Mercedes, Mercy, Ransom (b)

Molly

Pronunciation: \ ˈmä-lē \

Though many are familiar with Molly as a stand-alone name, it originated as a nickname for Mary, as did Polly. (It should also be noted that Molly has found decent use as a nickname for Margaret, though Margaret and Molly are unrelated). Though Molly doesn't have exclusively Irish use, it's almost always included in lists of Irish names and has — at least in America — a distinctly Irish feel.

Nickname: Moll

Variants: Mollie, Pollie, Polly

Feast day: September 12 (Most Holy Name of Mary)

See also: Molson

Molly in real life, literature, and/or culture

Molly is a name of note across categories, from literary characters such as Molly Bloom in James Joyce's _Ulysses_ and Molly Weasley in the _Harry Potter_ series, to songs like "Molly Malone" and "Good Golly, Miss Molly," to historical figures like "The Unsinkable Molly Brown" (who was actually born Margaret and called Maggie during her life, not being referred to as Molly until after her death), to modern actresses Molly Ringwald and Molly Shannon. I also have both a sister and sister-in-law with the given name Molly.

Montserrat

Pronunciation: \ män(t)-sə-'rat \

Montserrat is the name of a mountain in Spain, on which is located the Santa Maria de Montserrat monastery, which is a shrine to Our Lady of Montserrat (*Santa Maria de Montserrat* means "Holy Mary of Montserrat" in Spanish; she's also known as *Mare de Déu de Montserrat in Catalan*). This title refers to an image of Our Lady — one of the Black Madonnas, so called because of her dark skin — dating back to the 12th or 13th century. The *Virolai* is a hymn to Our Lady of Montserrat, and begins, *Rosa d'abril, Morena de la serra* ... ("Rose of April, dark lady of the mountain ..."), and so Our Lady of Montserrat is sometimes referred to as the April Rose.

Nicknames: Mont, Monny, Montse, Monxo, Muntsa, Rateta, Serra, Serrat, Tóna

Variant: Monserrat

Feast day: April 27 (Our Lady of Montserrat)

See also: Rose

Montserrat in real life, literature, and/or culture

With the equally Marian name Aranza, Montserrat and its variant Monserrat were the fastest-rising girls' names in America in 2014. Those who are familiar with *telenovelas* (Latin soap operas) likely recognized the names from TV; those who are familiar with Marian titles rejoiced at seeing Our Lady so well represented in a country whose use of the name Mary has been falling for a long time.

Morna

Pronunciation: \ ˈmȯr-nə \

While Morna isn't etymologically related to Mary, it needs to be included in this volume for personal reasons: It's my middle name, bestowed because my mom — who was determined to give all of her daughters a Marian name — saw Morna listed as an Irish variant of Mary in a name book when she was pregnant with me (1978).

When I started learning about name meanings and started reading name books and websites, I was never able to find Morna listed as an Irish form of Mary. I did discover that it's a form of Muirne, which was the name of Finn McCool's (Fionn mac Cumhail's) mother. Morna and Muirne are strikingly similar in appearance and sound to Maura/ Moira and Muire (which *are* actual Irish forms of Mary), which may be where the initial confusion came from. But I've always held that, in naming, intention almost always matters more than fact, and since my parents *intended* me to be named for Mother Mary, I am.

Furthermore, though Morna isn't a variant of Mary, a legitimate argument can be made that it can be considered Marian. Its meaning in Irish is sometimes listed as "beloved," which puts Morna in the good company of other names meaning "beloved" that have been included in this book (e.g., Amata, Annabel).

Variants: Muirne (Irish), Murna, Myrna

Feast day: September 12 (Most Holy Name of Mary)

See also: Amata, Amabilis (b), Annabel, Meryt

Natividad

Pronunciation: \ nä-tē-vē-ˈdäd \

Natividad is Spanish for "Nativity" or "birthday" (it actually derives from the Latin *natale domini*, which means, literally, "the birth of the Lord," that is, Christmas Day). Its Marian character is twofold: On one hand it relates to Our Lady's title "Our Lady of the Nativity," in her role as Jesus' mother; on the other it is connected to her own birth, celebrated as the Feast of the Nativity of Our Lady on September 8.

Nicknames: Nat, Natty, Tivi

Variants: Natalia (various), Natalie (various), Natalya (Russian), Natasha (Russian diminutive), Nathalie (French), Noella (French), Noelle (French)

Feast days: September 8 (Nativity of Our Lady)
December 25 (Christmas Day)

See also: Madonna, Theotokos (b)

Nazaret

Pronunciation: \ na-zə-ˈret \

Nazareth is the town Our Lady was born and grew up in; it's the town in which the Angel Gabriel visited her — the town in which her *fiat* and the Incarnation occurred. Our Lady of Nazareth is an ancient title under which she has long been venerated, and there is a miraculous statue of the Madonna and Child in Nazare, Portugal, which is said to

have been carved by St. Joseph and painted by St. Luke. Nazaret is a feminine name in Spanish and a masculine name in Armenian.

Variants: Nazareta (Romanian), Nazaretta (Italian), Nazret (Amharic)

Feast day: March 6 (Our Lady of Nazareth)

See also: Annunziata, Belén, Fiat, Gabriel (b), Gabriela, Joseph (b), Luke (b), Nazario (b), Nunzio (b)

Nieves

Pronunciation: \ ˈnye-ves \

From the Spanish word for "snow" (*nieve*), Nieves refers to the Marian title *Nuestra Señora de las Nieves* ("Our Lady of the Snows"), which is also another name for the Basilica of St. Mary Major (*Santa Maria Maggiore*) in Rome, built around the year 352 during the reign of Pope Liberius (352-366). Its location was chosen after the benefactors had a dream in which Our Lady requested her church to be built on a snow-covered hill, even though it was summer (August 4, 352). The next day, the miraculous snow was discovered to be blanketing Esquiline Hill. It is now the custom that every year on the feast of the Dedication of the Basilica of St. Mary Major (August 5), white rose petals are scattered from the dome of the Chapel of Our Lady at the end of Mass.

Nickname: Nia

Variants: Edurne (Basque), Neves (Portuguese), Nives (Italian), Snow (English)

Feast day: August 5 (Our Lady of the Snows, as well as the Feast of the Dedication of the Basilica of St. Mary Major)

See also: Biancamaria, Meritxell

Núria

Pronunciation: \ ˈnü-rē-ä \

The Valley of Núria in Catalonia, Spain is the home of a statue of Our Lady known in Catalan as *Mare de Dèu de Núria* ("Our Lady of Núria"). Tradition holds that St. Giles created the statue around the beginning of the eighth century and hid it in a cave when he was forced to flee persecution. Over 300 years later, a pilgrim named Amadéu had a dream about the image and began looking for it, and after seven years found it and brought it to the chapel he had built. Our Lady of Núria is still revered there, though the current statue dates back to the 12th or 13th century.

Variant: Nuria (no accent)

Feast day: September 8 (Our Lady of Núria)

Olivia

Pronunciation: \ ō-ˈliv-ē-ə, ə-ˈliv-ē-ə \

One of Mother Mary's titles is "Our Lady of the Olives," also known as Madonna of Olives, which makes any of the Oliv- names doable in her honor. Under this title, Our Lady has been compared to an olive tree in this verse in the book of Sirach: "Like a fair olive tree in the field" (Sir 24:14), and also remembered for a miraculous occurrence involving lightning in a town in France. Additionally, Our Lady of Peace (also known as Queen of Peace and Mother of Peace) is represented in art holding a dove and an olive branch, symbols of peace.

In a funny twist, though the names Oliva and Olive definitely mean "olive" and are therefore impeccably linked to Our Lady of the Olives, I decided to head this entry "Olivia," as it's currently the most popular and familiar of the Oliv- names. Although Olivia may or may not be etymologically related to "olive" (it could have arisen as a feminine variant of Oliver, which isn't related to "olive" [see Oliver]), if the name is bestowed with the intention of honoring Our Lady of Olives, I think it works quite well. Although there are alternate spellings of Olivia, like Alivia and Olyvia, the Olivia spelling most closely ties the name to the Marian title.

Nicknames: Lia, Liv, Livia, Livvy, Ollie, Via, Vivi

Variants: Oliva (Latin), Olivie (French), Olivette (French), Olyvia

Feast day: June 18 (Our Lady of Olives)

See also: Oliver (b), Paloma, Pace (b), Pax (b), Paz

Paderau

Pronunciation: \ ˈpä-dā-rā, pä-ˈde-rī \

There seems to be some disagreement over whether this Welsh word, which means "beads" or "rosary," can be (or is) used as a name. In my mind, since Rosary and Rosario are used as names, so can the word for it in other languages! Paderau can be used for a boy or a girl, and if it's too bold for a first name, it can make a really unusual and unique Marian middle.

Nicknames: Derry, Paddy, Rye

Feast day: October 7 (Our Lady of the Rosary)

See also: Bartolo (b), Cap (b), Paderau (b), Paidrín, Rosario (b), Rosary, Victor (b), Victoria

Paidrín

Pronunciation: \ pä-ˈdrēn \

Like Paderau, Paidrín is more familiar as a noun than a name — it's the Irish word for "rosary" — but I argue that any word for Rosary can be a name, and the Rosary always points back to Our Lady.

Nicknames: Dreen, Paddy, Reenie

Feast day: October 7 (Our Lady of the Rosary)

See also: Bartolo (b), Cap (b), Paderau, Paderau (b), Rosario (b), Rosary, Victor (b), Victoria

Paloma

Pronunciation: \ pəˈlōmə \

This beautiful Spanish name means "dove," and Our Lady is particularly honored under the title *La Virgen de la Paloma* ("The Virgin of the Dove") in Madrid, Spain. This title actually comes from a painting of Our Lady of Solitude (*Nuestra Señora de la Soledad*), which hangs in a church on the street called Paloma in Madrid and is referred to as *La Paloma*. The doves referred to in the Song of Songs are also understood to refer to Our Lady.

Nicknames: Pali, Palomita, Polly

Feast day: Holy Saturday (Our Lady of Solitude)

See also: Soledad

Paloma in real life, literature, and/or culture
The artist Pablo Picasso's daughter goes by Paloma (her given name is Anne Paloma, what a gorgeous — and very Marian — combination!).

Panagiota

Pronunciation: \ pä-nä-yō-tä \

This is a common Greek name for Our Lady, meaning "all holy," from *pan* meaning "all" and *hagios* meaning "holy." *The Catechism of the Catholic Church* notes:

> The Fathers of the Eastern tradition call the Mother of God "the All-Holy" (*Panagia*), and celebrate her as "free from any stain of sin, as though fashioned by the Holy Spirit and formed as a new creature."[32] By the grace of God Mary remained free of every personal sin her whole life long. (*CCC*, 493)

Nicknames: Betty, Giota, Nagia, Patty, Peggy, Penny, Toula, Yiota

Feast day: August 15 (Assumption)

See also: Panagiotis (b), Santamaria

Toula in real life, literature, and/or culture
Though Toula is given as a nickname for Panagiota, it should be clarified that the character of Toula in "My Big Fat Greek Wedding" actually had the given name Fotoula, which isn't related to Panagiota.

Paz

Pronunciation: \ ˈpäs, ˈpäz \

In Spanish, *paz* means "peace," and is used as a name specifically in honor of *Nuestra Señora de la Paz* ("Our Lady of Peace"), which is associated with a mysterious statue of Our Lady that inspired warring factions in El Salvador to stop fighting, both in the 17th and 19th centuries.

"Queen of Peace" is also one of the titles of Our Lady included in the Litany of Loreto.

Variant: Irene (Greek)

Feast days: July 9 (Our Lady, Queen of Peace)
November 21 (Our Lady of Peace, El Salvador)

See also: Olivia, Oliver (b), Paloma, Pace (b), Pax (b),
Regina, Reina, Reginald (b)

Paz in real life, literature, and/or culture
Spanish actress Paz Vega's given name is María Paz, so beautiful!

Pearl

Pronunciation: \ ˈpər(-ə)l \

Though Pearl is a variant of Margaret, since Margaret means "pearl" (Latin: *margarita*), Pearl can take its place as a Marian name through the fact that Our Lady is referred to as "Pearl of Virgins" in the Litany of Our Lady of Seven Sorrows.

Nicknames: Pearlie, Perlita

Variants: Perla (Italian, Spanish), Perle (French)

Feast day: September 15 (Our Lady of Sorrows)

See also: Addolorata, Daisy, Dolores, Pieta, Virginia

Perpetua

Pronunciation: \pər-ˈpe-chə-wə\

From the Latin for "perpetual, continuous," Perpetua refers to Our Lady of Perpetual Help, also known as Our Mother of Perpetual Help and Our Lady of Perpetual Succour. The icon of Our Lady of Perpetual Help was entrusted to the Redemptorist Order in 1866 by Pope Pius IX, who instructed them to "make her known."[33]

Nicknames: Peppy, Pet, Pia, Pip, Pippa, Poppy

Feast day: June 27 (Our Lady of Perpetual Help)

See also: Auxilio, Auxilio (b), Socorro

Perpetua in real life, literature, and/or culture
Saint Perpetua was martyred in Carthage, North Africa, in the be-

ginning of the third century. She was a noblewoman, and her maid Felicity was also martyred with her.

Pia

Pronunciation: \ ˈpē-ə \

Pia is the feminine form of Pius, which means "pious, devout, dutiful." In the *Salve Regina*, Our Lady is called *pia*, which is translated in the English version as "loving."

Feast day: September 12 (Most Holy Name of Mary)

See also: Piedad, Pio (b), Pius (b)

***Pia* in real life, literature, and/or culture**

Pia Toscano was a contestant on Season 10 of "American Idol." All of the popes and Sts. Pius, as well as St. Pio of Pietrelcina, have the male variant of this name.

Piedad

Pronunciation: \ pē-ə-ˈdäd \

Piedad is a Spanish name stemming from the Marian title *Nuestra Señora de la Piedad* ("Our Lady of Pity" or "Piety"), which is connected to Our Lady of Sorrows.

Nickname: Pia

Feast day: September 15 (Our Lady of Sorrows)

See also: Addolorata, Angustias, Dolores, Iris, Ivy, Pia, Pierce (b), Pieta, Simeon (b), Tristan (b)

Pieta

Pronunciation: \ pē-ˈā-tä, ˈpyä-tä, pē-ā-ˈtä \

Pietá is the Italian word for "pity," and refers specifically to artwork depicting Mary holding the dead body of Jesus. It's an unusual and beautiful way to honor the sorrow of Our Lady with a name.

Nicknames: Ada, Eta, Pia

Feast day: September 15 (Our Lady of Sorrows)

See also: Addolorata, Angustias, Cruz, Cruz (b), Dolores, Iris, Ivy, Piedad, Pierce (b), Simeon (b), Tristan (b)

Pilar

Pronunciation: \ pē-ˈlär \

The Spanish title *María del Pilar* ("Mary of the Pillar") has the distinction of referring to what's considered Our Lady's first apparition in

history — she is said to have appeared to St. James in Spain in the first half of the first century, while she was still alive and residing in Jerusalem.

Nickname: Lara, Pili

Feast day: October 12 (Our Lady of the Pillar)

Presentación

Pronunciation: \ pre-sen-tä-ˈsyōn (Spanish — Latin America), pre-sen-tä-ˈthyōn (Spanish — Spain) \

Though we are familiar the with the Presentation of the Baby Jesus in the Temple (the Fourth Joyful Mystery), the Spanish name Presentación is characterized as a Marian name in the sources in which I found it, as it refers to the Presentation of Mary in the Temple when she was a child.

Feast day: November 21 (Presentation of Mary)

Primrose

Pronunciation: \ ˈprim-rōz \

The name of the primrose flower comes from the Latin *prima rosa* (first rose), which of course is Marian enough as it is, but the primrose has also been known as Our Lady's Frills.

Nicknames: Posey, Posy, Prim, Rosey, Rosie

Feast day: October 7 (Our Lady of the Rosary)

See also: Rose

Primrose in real life, literature, and/or culture

Rare names are the most susceptible to having a well-known association stick. The lovely "Primrose" has never been in the top 1,000 names in the U.S., but it's currently well known as the name of a main character in the *Hunger Games* series.

Prouille

Pronunciation: \ ˈprü-ē, prü-ˈē \

The town of Prouille in France is the location of St. Dominic's vision during which, tradition tells us, Our Lady gave him the Rosary — indeed, Prouille has been referred to as the "cradle of the rosary" by Pope Pius XI.[34]

With Prouille's possible nickname of Pru, which is shared by the more familiar name Prudence, I think this Marian place name is very doable.

Nickname: Pru

Feast day: October 7 (Our Lady of the Rosary)

See also: Dominic (b), Paderau, Paderau (b), Paidrín, Rosario (b), Rosary

Pureza

Pronunciation: \ pü-ˈrā-zə \

Pureza is Spanish for "pure" and refers to Our Lady of Purity; the Theatine Fathers have a special devotion to Our Lady under this title.

Nickname: Reza

Feast day: October 16 (Purity of the Blessed Virgin Mary)

See also: Biancamaria, Concepción, Edelweiss, Immaculata, Ivory, Ivory (b), Lily

Purificación

Pronunciation: \ pü-rē-fē-kä-ˈsyōn (Spanish — Latin America), pü-rē-fē-kä-ˈthyōn (Spanish — Spain) \

Though the "Presentación" entry referred to the Presentation of Mary in the Temple as a child, the Spanish name Purificación comes from the Marian title *Nuestra Señora de la Purificación* ("Our Lady of the Purification") and refers to the post-birth ritual purification of Mary in the Temple, 40 days after giving birth to Jesus; it's celebrated on the same day as the Presentation of the Baby Jesus in the Temple (Fourth Joyful Mystery of the Rosary).

Nickname: Puri

Feast day: February 2 (Purification of Mary, also known as Candlemas)

See also: Candelaria, Candelario (b), Presentación

Regina

Pronunciation: \ re-ˈjē-nä, re-ˈgē-nä, re-ˈjī-nä \

Our Lady is referred to as *Regina* (Latin for "queen") of many things, including Queen of Heaven, Queen of the Angels, Queen of the Apostles, Queen of the World, Queen of Ireland, and Queen of Peace. Regina is one of the most identifiably Marian names and, I would argue, almost exclusively Catholic in use.

Nicknames: Geena, Gena, Genie, Gina, Jeannie, Ina, Reggie

Variants: Rayna (Bulgarian), Regine (various), Reginette (Italian), Reina (Spanish), Reine (French), Reyna (Spanish), Ríona (Irish), Ríonach (Irish)

Feast day: August 22 (Queenship of Mary)

See also: Candace, Reina, Reginald (b)

Reina

Pronunciation: \ ˈrā-nə \

Though *Reina* means "queen," just like the previous entry (Regina), I thought it deserved its own entry as it has such a different feel. Not only can it be used on its own, but it's often the call name for the beautiful compound name Maria Reina (common among Hispanic families).

Variants: Rayna (Bulgarian), Regina (various), Regine (various), Reginette (Italian), Reine (French), Reyna (Spanish), Ríona (Irish), Ríonach (Irish)

Feast day: August 22 (Queenship of Mary)

See also: Candace, Regina, Reginald (b)

Remedios

Pronunciation: \ re-ˈmā-dyōs \

Another beautiful Spanish name, Remedios comes from the Marian title *Nuestra Señora de los Remedios* ("Our Lady of the Remedies," also known as "Our Lady of Good Remedy" or "Good Remedies"), a title under which she is the patroness of the Order of the Holy Trinity (Trinitarians), which was founded in the 12th century to ransom Christian captives. Devotion to her — as well as a well-known statue of Our Lady of Good Remedy — was brought to Mexico by the *conquistadores*, and the Sanctuary of the Virgin of Los Remedios is in Mexico's Los Remedios National Park.

Nicknames: Madie, Reme, Remy

Feast days: September 1 (Virgin of the Remedies,
celebrated in Mexico)
October 8 (Our Lady of Good Remedy,
celebrated by the Trinitarians)

See also: Ransom (b)

Remedios in real life, literature, and/or culture
Artist Remedios Varo (d. 1963) was born María de los Remedios. The name Remedios is also borne by several characters in Gabriel García Márquez's book *One Hundred Years of Solitude* (1967).

Reyes

Pronunciation: \ ˈrā-yes \

Included in the beautiful Spanish Marian titles is *La Virgen de los Reyes* ("The Virgin of the Kings") or *Nuestra Señora de los Reyes* ("Our Lady of the Kings"). It refers to a 13th-century miraculous sculpture of Our Lady holding the infant Jesus, commissioned by the second wife of King Ferdinand III of Castile and León in Spain and created, as tradition holds, by angels in disguise. When the king was prostrate before it one night in anguish over the setbacks his army was experiencing in their attempts to lay siege to Muslim-controlled Seville, Our Lady spoke to him and assured him of his eventual success, which he achieved not long after. The statue still resides in the Cathedral of Seville above the incorrupt body of King Ferdinand III, who was canonized in 1671 by Pope Clement X.[35] The name Reyes is used for both girls and boys in honor of Our Lady of the Kings.

Nickname: Rey

Feast day: August 15 (Our Lady of the Kings, as well as the Assumption of Our Lady)

Rocío

Pronunciation: \ rō-ˈsē-ō (Spanish — Latin America),
rō-ˈthē-ō (Spanish — Spain) \

Rocío means "dew" in Spanish, and refers to Our Lady under the title *Nuestra Señora del Rocío* ("Our Lady of the Dew"). She's been venerated under this title in southern Spain since the 13th century, and is also sometimes called *La Blanca Paloma* ("The White Dove"), *La Reina de la Marismas* ("Queen of the Marshes"), *Nuestra Señora de las Rocinas* ("Our Lady of the Rocinas," referring to the name of the place before it was called El Rocío), and Our Lady of Pentecost, since the feast of Our Lady of the Dew is celebrated on Pentecost.

Nicknames: Chio, Ro, Rochi, Rosy

Feast day: Pentecost Sunday (seventh Sunday after Easter)

See also: Biancamaria, Paloma, Reina

Rosary

Pronunciation: \ ˈrō-zə-rē, ˈrōz-rē \

Not only does the word "rosary" come from the idea of "a crown of roses for Our Lady," but Mary is also revered under the title Our Lady of the Rosary. Though an unusual pick for a first name, its similarity to the other Rose names and its nickname possibility of "Rosie" make Rosary a lovely choice.

Nicknames: Ro, Rose, Rosey, Rosie

Variants: Paderau, Paidrín

Feast day: October 7 (Our Lady of the Rosary)

See also: Bartolo (b), Cap (b), Dominic (b), Paderau, Paderau (b), Paidrín, Prouille, Rosario (b), Rose, Victor (b), Victoria

Rosary in real life, literature, and/or culture

I did a baby name consultation for a mother who wondered if Rosary was too strange for a first name. My opinion was that it wasn't — on the contrary, what an amazing name for a little Catholic girl! The parents did indeed end up naming their little girl Rosary.[36] I subsequently learned that Rosary is not an uncommon first name in the New Orleans area.[37]

Rose

Pronunciation: \ ˈrōz \

Roses are associated with Our Lady in so many ways, from the golden roses on her feet at Lourdes to the roses spilling from St. Juan Diego's tilma in Guadalupe, to her titles (e.g., "Mystical Rose," "Golden Rose," "Queen of Ireland"), to the Rosary itself, whose name comes from the idea of a crown of roses for Our Lady. She is also identified as the "rose of Sharon" from the Song of Songs (2:1). As happens with Mary, Rose is often added to other names and words to make lovely variations like Roseanne, Rosangela, Rosemary, and Primrose.

Nicknames: Rosey, Rosie

Variants: Rhosyn (Welsh), Róisín (Irish), Rosa (various), Rosabel (English), Rosaleen (English, Irish), Rosalia (various), Rosalie (French), Rosalind (English), Roselle (French), Rosette (French), Rosetta (Italian), Rosheen (Irish), Rosita (Italian)

Feast day: September 12 (Most Holy Name of Mary)

See also: Aurea, Guadalupe, Guadalupe (b), Juan Diego (b), Lourdes, Meritxell, Montserrat, Paderau, Paderau (b), Paidrín, Primrose, Rosario (b), Rosary, Rosemary, Royce (b), Sharon, Tilma

Rosemary

Pronunciation: \ ˈrōz-mer-ē \

You could think of Rosemary as either a combination of the names Rose and Mary, or as a reference to the herb by the same name (*Rosemarinus officinalis*), which comes from the Latin *ros marinus* ("dew of the sea"). Like the juniper tree, it's said to have sheltered the Holy Family during their flight into Egypt, and there are stories that say its blue flowers came either from Our Lady drying the clothes of little Jesus on the rosemary bush, or from drying her own blue mantle on it. Rosemary is said to signify the faithfulness of Our Lady.

Nicknames: Ro, Romy, Romey, Rose, Rosey, Rosie, Rory

Variant: Rosemarie (various)

Feast day: September 12 (Most Holy Name of Mary)

See also: Blue, Blue (b), Juniper, Juniper (b), Rocío, Romero (b), Rose, Royce (b)

Rosemary in real life, literature, and/or culture
Though I still come across parents who are put off by the name
Rosemary because of the 1968 movie "Rosemary's Baby," the
association seems to be nearly gone, as I've seen many, many more
babies given this beautiful Marian name in recent years.

S

Salette

Pronunciation: \ sä-ˈlet \

This lovely name comes from the Marian title "Our Lady of La Salette," which refers to an apparition of Our Lady to two children in La Salette-Fallavaux, France in 1846. Since Our Lady was crying, this apparition is closely associated with her title "Our Lady of Sorrows." Though I've never seen Salette used for a girl in real life, one of my readers had considered it for a daughter.

Nicknames: Etta, Ette, Etty, Sally

Feast day: September 19 (Our Lady of La Salette)

See also: Addolorata, Akita, Angustias, Banneux (b), Beauraing (b), Dolores, Fatima, Guadalupe, Guadalupe (b), Kibeho, Kibeho (b), Knock (b), Lourdes, Piedad, Pierce (b), Pieta, Simeon (b), Tepeyac (b), Walsingham (b)

Salud, Salut

Pronunciation: \ sä-ˈlüd (Salud), sä-ˈlüt (Salut) \

Nuestra Señora de la Salud ("Our Lady of Health") is a title known in both Mexico and Spain, referring to a 16th-century apparition and image of Our Lady in Mexico, and the intercession of Our Lady that resulted in the halting of a 17th-century epidemic of yellow fever in Spain.

Mare de Déu de la Salut ("Our Lady of Health") is a Catalan title by which Our Lady is revered as patroness in Algemesí, Spain, dating back to the 13th century. And "Health of the sick" is one of Our Lady's titles in the Litany of Loreto.

Both Salud and Salut have traditionally been given to girls in honor of our Blessed Mother.

Nicknames: Lulu, Sali

Feast days: Last Saturday in May (Our Lady of Health, Alcantarilla, Spain)
September 8 (Our Lady of Health, Algemesí, Spain)
December 8 (Our Lady of Health, Mexico)

Santamaria

Pronunciation: \ sän-tä-mä-ˈrē-a \

As far as I can tell, Santamaria — which means "holy Mary" or "St. Mary" in Spanish and Italian — is mostly known as a last name, but I think it would be very natural as a first name, especially since names meaning "saint," "holy," or "St. So-and-so" are not uncommon as first names (e.g., Saint, Santina/o, Sancha/o, Santiago, St. John, Sinclair, Toussaint).

Nicknames: Maria, Mia, Ree, Ria, Sancha, Santa, Santina

Variants: Mariasancha (Spanish), Sanchamaria (Spanish), Santa Maria (Italian, Spanish)

Feast day: September 12 (Most Holy Name of Mary)

See also: Panagiota, Panagiotis (b)

Seraphina

Pronunciation: \ ser-ə-ˈfēn-ə \

This lovely name refers to the seraphim, the order of angels who "stand before God as ministering servants in the heavenly court,"[38] and gets its Marian character from two of Our Lady's titles: "Our Lady of the Angels" and "Queen of the Angels."

Nicknames: Fia, Fina, Sera, Sofie/Sophie, Sunny

Variants: Serafina, Seraphita

Feast day: August 2 (Our Lady of the Angels)

See also: Angela, Angelo (b), Candace, Regina, Reginald (b), Reina, Seraphim (b)

Sharon

Pronunciation: \ ˈsher-en, ˈshar-en \

Our Lady's title *Rosa Mystica* ("Mystical Rose") from the Litany of Loreto stems from the "rose of Sharon" referenced in the Song of Songs (2:1), which is traditionally understood to refer to Mary. In the Old Testament, the Sharon plain in Israel was known for its fertility and beauty.

Nickname: Shari

Variants: Sharona, Sharron, Sharyn

Feast day: September 12 (Most Holy Name of Mary)

See also: Rose

Socorro

Pronunciation: \ sə-ˈkȯr-ō \

Our Lady of Perpetual Succour, also known as Our Lady of Perpetual Help, is *Nuestra Señora del Perpetuo Socorro* in Spanish. The icon of Our Lady of Perpetual Help is one of the most well known, and was entrusted to the Redemptorist Order by Pope Pius IX in 1866, who told them to "make her known."[39]

Nicknames: Cora, Cori, Corra, Corry

Variant: Socorra

Feast day: June 27 (Our Lady of Perpetual Help)

See also: Auxilio, Auxilio (b), Perpetua

Soledad

Pronunciation: \ ˈsō-le-dad, sō-lā-ˈdäd (Spanish — Latin America), sō-lā-ˈt͟hät͟h (Spanish — Spain) \

This beautiful Spanish name means "solitude," and comes from the Marian title *Nuestra Señora de Soledad* ("Our Lady of Solitude"), which refers to the solitude of Our Lady while Jesus was in the tomb. María de la Soledad is not uncommon as a given name in Spanish-speaking families, and Marisol is sometimes used as a nickname for it.

Nicknames: Marisol (for Maria de la Soledad), Sol, Sole

Feast day: Holy Saturday (Our Lady of Solitude)

See also: Paloma

***Soledad* in real life, literature, and/or culture**
Journalist and former CNN host Soledad O'Brien's given name is
María de la Soledad Teresa O'Brien.

Sophia

Pronunciation: \ sō-ˈfē-ə, sōˈfī-ə (British English) \

Sophia means "wisdom" in Greek, and can refer to Our Lady's titles
"Our Lady of Wisdom" and "Seat" or "Throne of Wisdom" (in Latin:
sedes sapientiae).

Nicknames: Fia, Sophie, Sophy

Variants: Sofia (various), Sofie (various), Sofija (various),
Sofiya (various), Sofya (Russian), Sonja (Scandinavian),
Sonje (German), Sonya (Russian diminutive), Wisdom,
Zofia (Polish), Zosia (Polish diminutive)

Feast day: June 8 (Our Lady, Seat of Wisdom)

Stella

Pronunciation: \ ˈste-lə \

The name Stella has two lovely connections to Our Lady: one is her title *Stella Maris* ("Star of the Sea," sometimes also seen as *Maris Stella*); the other is her title *Madonna della Stella* ("Our Lady of the Star").

Variants: Estelle (French), Estela (Portuguese, Spanish), Estrella (Spanish), Maristela (Portuguese, Spanish), Maristella (Italian), Stella Maris, Stellamaris

Feast days: September 27 (Our Lady, Star of the Sea)
Easter Monday (Madonna della Stella, Puglia, Italy)
Sunday following Easter (Madonna della Stella, Los Angeles, CA)

See also: Ave, Demaris, Marina, Maris

Sterpeta

Pronunciation: \ stər-ˈpet-ə \

This rare Italian name is derived from the Marian title *Madonna dello Sterpeto* ("Our Lady of Sterpeto"), where *sterpeto* refers to "scrub land." A shrine in Barletta, Italy in honor of Our Lady of Sterpeto houses a Byzantine image of the Madonna and Child, which dates back to the 17th century, and was discovered at the same time that the plague, which was particularly affecting the city, began to wane.

Nicknames: Peta, Steta, Stetta

Feast days: May 8 (Our Lady of Sterpeto, liturgical feast day)
Second Sunday of July (Our Lady of Sterpeto, patronal feast day)

Susanna

Pronunciation: \ sü-ˈza-nə \

I debated whether or not to include Susanna in this volume, but I ultimately decided to do so for several reasons. First, it means both "lily" and "rose" in Hebrew, both of which are connected to Our Lady. Second, as I noted in the entry for Assumpta, there has already been an unofficial connection created between the very Marian name Assumpta and the name Susan, as there's a history of Susan being used as an anglicization of Assumpta. Finally, the name Azucena, which I discussed earlier in this book, is the Spanish name for the Madonna lily, and is said to be etymologically related to Susanna.

Nicknames: Anna, Annie, Sanna, Sookie, Sue, Suki, Susie, Zanna, Zuzu

Variants: Shoshana (Hebrew), Sósanna (Irish), Susan (English), Susana (Portuguese, Spanish), Susannah

Feast day: August 15 (Assumption)

See also: Assumpta, Assunto (b), Azucena, Lily, Rose

Suyapa

Pronunciation: \ sü-ˈyä-pä \

This lovely name is from another of Our Lady's beautiful Spanish titles: *Nuestra Señora de Suyapa*, where Suyapa is the name of a town in Honduras. Under this title, she is greatly revered in Honduras, where there is a miraculous image and basilica of Our Lady of Suyapa.

Nicknames: Su, Sue, Supa, Susie, Suya

Feast day: February 3 (Our Lady of Suyapa)

Tilma

Pronunciation: \ ˈtilmə \

The word *tilma* is well known and loved by Catholics — it's the name of the garment worn by St. Juan Diego during his visions of Our Lady of Guadalupe, and it's the garment from which tumbled the miraculous roses when he brought Our Lady's message to his bishop, and on which the miraculous image of Our Lady of Guadalupe appeared and remains to this day.

Though I've not seen Tilma used as a given name, I think it could easily become so, especially given its similarity to the established female name Thelma, and especially Thelma's Portuguese variant, Telma.

Nickname: Tilly

Feast day: December 12 (Our Lady of Guadalupe)

See also: Achiropita, Juan Diego (b), Guadalupe, Guadalupe (b), Mantle (b), Rose, Tepeyac (b), Veil

Treille, Trielle

Pronunciation: \ ˈtrā, ˈtrā-yə (Treille); trē-ˈel (Trielle) \

I first became aware of the word *trielle* in Fr. Calloway's book *Champions of the Rosary*, in which he told about a 13th century confraternity called the Trielle, whose membership contained "several pious ladies who offered 'Psalters of Our Lady' [an old name for the Rosary] in lieu of money or candles."[40]

In researching more about the word *trielle* and whether it could be an entry in this book, I discovered a Marian mystery! There are references to *Notre Dame de la Trielle,* said to be the name of a church in Lille, France, in various old books including the *Americanized Encyclopaedia Britannica* (1893), *The Catholic Encyclopedia* (1912), and *Vanished Halls and Cathedrals of France* (1917),[41] but with no further information given than its name. Upon further research, I've come to suspect it may be a repeated typo of the name *Notre Dame de la Treille* ("Our Lady of the Trellis," also referred to as Our Lady of the Vine), after which the Lille Cathedral is named — also known as the Basilica of Notre Dame de la Treille (Our Lady of the Trellis refers to a miraculous 12th century statue of Our Lady).

I think both names are doable as lovely, unusual options for girls, and both point to Our Lady, whether through Our Lady of the Trellis or the pious ladies who offered rosaries.

Feast day: June 14 (Our Lady of the Trellis)

Veil

Pronunciation: \ ˈvāl \

Our Lady always wears a veil, both in her apparitions and in artistic renditions. There is a piece of silk called the *Voile de la Vierge* ("Veil of the Blessed Virgin," also known as the *Sancta Camisia*) at the Cathedral of Our Lady of Chartres in Chartres, France, which pious tradition holds was Our Lady's veil.

Additionally, Our Lady of Mercy (also known as the *Madonna della Misericordia*) is associated with images of the faithful taking refuge under her cloak, also known as her veil or mantle.

Feast day: September 12 (Most Holy Name of Mary)

See also: Mantle (b), Mercy

Veil in real life, literature, and/or culture

I would not normally have thought of Veil as a given name but for two recent occurrences: the first was the sound-alike name Vale bestowed as a first name upon the baby daughter of the "Today Show" co-anchor Savannah Guthrie; the second was discovering that a mother I know had given the name Veil to her daughter as one of her middle names, specifically "after the Holy Protection of Our Lady, since Mary's veil is known as a symbol of her motherly protection and care."[42]

Veronica

Pronunciation: \ və-ˈrä-ni-kə \

Though Veronica is an existing girl's name unrelated to Our Lady, *Veronica* is also a genus of flowering plant. There are several that were called by Marian names in medieval times: *Veronica chamaedrys* was known as Our Lady's Resting Place, *Veronica maritima* as Lady's Faith, and *Veronica officinalis* as Lady's Plant (according to Vincenzina Krymow in her book *Mary's Flowers: Gardens, Legends & Meditations*, the "name 'Lady' in plants is almost always a post-Reformation contraction of 'Our Lady.'")[43]

Nicknames: Nica, Nicki, Ronnie, Roni, Vee, Vera, Vero, Via, Vivi

Feast day: September 12 (Most Holy Name of Mary)

See also: Faith

Victoria

Pronunciation: \ vik-ˈtȯr-ē-ə \

Our Lady of Victory is another name for Our Lady of the Rosary, and commemorates the victory of the Christian army against the Ottoman forces at the Battle of Lepanto in 1571, during which Pope Pius V had asked all of Europe to pray the Rosary and ask Our Lady to intercede for the Christian forces during the battle.

Nicknames: Cora, Cori, Ria, Tia, Tori, Toria, Via, Vic, Vick, Vicki, Vicky

Variants: Victoire (French), Viktoria (German, Scandinavian), Viktorija (various), Vitória (Portuguese), Vittoria (Italian), Wiktoria (Polish)

Feast day: October 7 (Our Lady of the Rosary)

See also: Paderau, Paderau (b), Paidrín, Pius (b), Rosario (b), Rosary, Victor (b)

Violet

Pronunciation: \ ˈvī-(ə-)lət \

The violet flower (*Viola odorata*) has been called Our Lady's Modesty, and has also been considered to represent her humility.

Nicknames: Lettie, Letty, Lola, Vi, Vio

Variants: Viola (various), Violette (French), Violeta (various), Violetta (Italian, Russian)

Feast day: September 12 (Most Holy Name of Mary)

Virginia

Pronunciation: \ vər-ˈji-nyə, vər-ˈji-nē-ə \

The name Virginia points to the perpetual virginity of Our Lady, which the Church explains thusly:

> The deepening of faith in the virginal motherhood led the Church to confess Mary's real and perpetual virginity even in the act of giving birth to the Son of God made man.[44] In fact, Christ's birth "did not diminish his mother's virginal

integrity but sanctified it."[45] And so the liturgy of the Church celebrates Mary as *Aeiparthenos*, the "Ever-virgin."[46]

Against this doctrine the objection is sometimes raised that the Bible mentions brothers and sisters of Jesus.[47] The Church has always understood these passages as not referring to other children of the Virgin Mary. In fact James and Joseph, "brothers of Jesus," are the sons of another Mary, a disciple of Christ, whom St. Matthew significantly calls "the other Mary."[48] They are close relations of Jesus, according to an Old Testament expression.[49] (*CCC*, 499-500)

Nicknames: Geena, Gena, Gigi, Gina, Ginger, Ginna, Ginnie, Ginny, Jinny, Virgee, Virgie

Variants: Verginia, Virginie (French)

Feast day: September 12 (Most Holy Name of Mary)

See also: Beauraing (b), Holly, Pureza

Visitación

Pronunciation: \ vē-zē-tä-ˈsyōn, bē-zē-tä-ˈsyōn (Spanish — Latin America), bē-zē-tä-ˈthyōn (Spanish — Spain) \

Referring to the Visitation of Our Lady to her cousin Elizabeth (Second Joyful Mystery of the Rosary), during which the unborn John the Baptist leapt for joy at being in the presence of his unborn Savior, Visitación is a beautiful Spanish name full of Marian and pro-life meaning.

Nicknames: Bee, Busy, Vee, Visi, Vita, Tasi

Variant: Ikerne (Basque)

Feast day: May 31 (Visitation of the Blessed Virgin Mary)

See also: Elizabeth, Iker (b), John (b), Magnificat

Vita

Pronunciation: \ ˈvē-tə \

In the *Salve Regina*, Our Lady is referred to as *vita, dulcedo, et spes nostra* ("our life, our sweetness, and our hope").

Nickname: Vee

Feast day: September 12 (Most Holy Name of Mary)

See also: Dulcie, Hope

Zinnia

Pronunciation: \ ˈzi-nē-ə, ˈzi-nyə \

The zinnia flower (*Zinnia peruviana*) was known as Little Mary in medieval times.

Nicknames: Zee, Zin, Zinni

Feast day: September 12 (Most Holy Name of Mary)

Names for boys

I think it's safe to say that most people would assume a book of Marian names would be a book of female names, but I've compiled here a list of male names that I think can be considered names that honor Our Blessed Mother. Many of the names are not obviously Marian, but when the right intention is behind their choosing — that is, the intention of choosing the name because of its connection to Our Lady — then their Marian character is indeed brought to the fore, and the boy or man is blessed with a name that will call to mind, for him and/ or for his parents, the Mother of Our Lord.

As with all the names in this book, the list is a subjective one. I've included all the male names I think are connected to Mary adequately enough that they can be considered Marian, but I've even been selective within this list. For example, Juan Diego seems obviously Marian to me — when I think of St. Juan Diego, I think of Our Lady appearing to him in Guadalupe. Rodrigo, however, does not seem Marian enough — even though Rodrigo de Baltzátegui received a vision of Our Lady in the 15th century (see Ainhoa and Aranza) — and so I have not included Rodrigo in the list. However, were someone to choose the name Rodrigo specifically because of its Marian connections, I do think Our Lady would be well pleased.

For each entry, I've included all the same information as is found in the girls' section: name; pronunciation; commentary; variant(s) (though I didn't include variants unrelated to the Marian aspect of the entry, e.g., Peter for Pierce); nickname(s); feast day(s); and "see also" names. Note that I've included the feast day of the Marian title or apparition to which the name refers, as well as the feast day of a saint who bears the name, where appropriate (a change from the girls' section, and another attempt to show the viability of these names for boys by pointing to actual male bearers of the names). And I've included real-life examples of names here and there.

As noted in the girls' section about names related to purported apparitions of Our Lady: Only a handful of apparitions have received formal approval from the Church, yet there are many, many names in this book that relate to pious traditions surrounding local apparitions. The inclusion of those names in this book is no comment on their validity; rather, I sought only to present all the names I could find that are bestowed by parents in honor of Our Lady.

Alan

Pronunciation: \ ˈa-lən \

The Marian character of the name Alan comes from Blessed Alan de la Roche (also known as Alain de la Roche, Alan de Rupe, Alano de la Roca, and Alanus [de] Rupe), a 15th-century Dominican who is listed as one of the 26 main "Champions of the Rosary" in Fr. Calloway's book of the same name. Fr. Calloway writes:

> Blessed Alan's love for Mary was so intense that, like many other chivalric saints, he was given the title "new spouse of Mary." His love for the Virgin of virgins was so pure and virtuous that he was considered another St. Joseph ... in his visions, Bl. Alan was even given a necklace made of Mary's hair and presented with a ring that symbolized the spiritual marriage existing between himself and the Virgin. In one of his visions, Mary appeared to him and placed the ring on his finger herself.[50]

Nickname: Al

Variants: Alain (French), Alano (Spanish), Alanus (Latin), Allan, Allen, Allyn, Alun (Welsh)

Feast days: September 8 (Blessed Alan de la Roche)
October 7 (Our Lady of the Rosary)

See also: Joseph

Alphonsus

Pronunciation: \ al-ˈfän-səs \

Saint Alphonsus Liguori, Doctor of the Church, whose given name included that of Our Lady (Alphonsus Maria Antony John Cosmas Damian Michael Gaspard de Liguori), and who was born at Marianella, Italy (Marianella has its own entry in this volume), also wrote "the most printed book on the Virgin Mary in the history of the Church: *The Glories of Mary* … It is truly a Mariological masterpiece … [he] became one of the most important Marian authors of the 18th century."[51]

Nicknames: Al, Lon, Lonnie, Phonse, Phonsie, Phonsey

Variants: Alfonso (Spanish, Italian), Alonzo (Italian), Alphonse (French)

Feast days: August 1 (St. Alphonsus Liguori)
October 7 (Our Lady of the Rosary)

See also: Marianella

***Phonse/Phonsey* in real life, literature, and/or culture**
I have a friend whose given name, like his dad's, is Alphonse Joseph. He goes by Phonse or Phonsey, as did his dad, who was a first generation Italian-American.

Amabilis

Pronunciation: \ əˈmä-bə-lis \

Amabilis is a Latin word meaning "lovable," and is part of the Marian title *Mater Amabilis* ("Mother Most Amiable" or "Mother Most Lovable"). It's also the name of a couple of early male saints.

Nicknames: Abe, Bill, Billy

Variants: Aimable (French), Amable (French)

Feast days: January 1 (Mary, Mother of God)
November 1 (St. Amabilis of Auvergne)

See also: Amata (g), Annabel (g), Kibeho, Kibeho (g), Meryt (g), Morna (g)

Aimable in real life, literature, and/or culture
Immaculée Ilibagiza, who survived the Rwandan genocide and now writes and speaks about Our Lady's apparitions in Kibeho, has a brother Aimable — the only other member of her family to survive the genocide.

Angelo

Pronunciation: \ ˈan-jə-lō \

The name Angelo refers to the angels, and as Our Lady is Queen of the Angels, I think this name — and all of the Angel- variants — can be considered Marian.

Variants: Angel (various), Ángel (Spanish), Angelino (Italian, Spanish), Angelus (Latin), Engel (German)

Feast day: August 2 (Feast of Our Lady Queen of Angels)

See also: Angela (g), Angelus, Candace, Regina (g), Reina (g), Reginald, Seraphina (g), Seraphim

Angel- names in real life, literature, and/or culture
Our new St. Pope John XXIII's pre-papal name was Angelo, and the main male character in Thomas Hardy's novel *Tess of the d'Urbervilles* is named Angel Clare.

Angelus

Pronunciation: \ ˈan-jə-ləs \

Angelus is an Angel- variant like Angelo above, being the Latin form of the name, but I've decided it merits its own entry since it has the added "oomph" of also being the name of the beautiful Marian devotion called the *Angelus*. Dennis Emmons explains:

> Among our many Catholic devotions, few are more beautiful or have been contemplated more often than the Angelus. Designed to commemorate the mystery of the Incarna-

tion and pay homage to Mary's role in salvation history, it has long been part of Catholic life. Around the world, three times every day, the faithful stop whatever they are doing and with the words "The Angel of the Lord declared unto Mary" begin this simple yet beautiful prayer.[52]

Feast day: March 25 (Annunciation)

See also: Angela (g), Angelo, Annunziata (g), Fiat (g), Gabriel, Gabriela (g), Nunzio, Seraphim, Seraphina (g)

Angelus in real life, literature, and/or culture

The beautiful painting "The Angelus" (_L'Angélus_ in French) by Jean-François Millet, completed in 1859, depicts a man and a woman taking a break from farming to pray the _Angelus_. Millet is reported as having said, "The idea for _The Angelus_ came to me because I remembered that my grandmother, hearing the church bell ringing while we were working in the fields, always made us stop work to say the Angelus prayer for the poor departed very religiously and with cap in hand."[53]

Anselm

Pronunciation: \ 'an-selm \

Saint Anselm of Canterbury is a Doctor of the Church, and while he's specifically referred to as the Father of Scholasticism, at least one source argues that he "deserves to be called a great Marian Doctor"

because of his devotion to and writings on Our Lady (*Cur Deus Homo* [Why God Became Man] and *De Conceptu Virginali et Originali Peccato* [The Virgin Conception and Original Sin]).[54] (I've also seen Anselm considered as a way to name a boy in honor of Our Lady's mother, St. Anne.)

Nicknames: Ace, Anse, Elmo

Variants: Anselme (French), Anselmi (Finnish), Anselmo (various)

Feast days: September 12 (Most Holy Name of Mary)
April 21 (St. Anselm of Canterbury)

See also: Anna (g)

Assunto

Pronunciation: \ ä-ˈsün-tō \

Assunto is the male variant of the Italian feminine name Assunta, which refers to the Assumption of Our Lady.

Nicknames: Ace, Sunto, Tony

Variants: Assundo (Italian), Assuntino (Italian)

Feast day: August 15 (Assumption)

See also: Assumpta (g), Susanna (g)

***Assundo* in real life, literature, and/or culture**
One of my blog readers shared that her grandfather's name was
"Assundo after the Assumption ... [her grandparents named one of
their daughters] Suzanne after my grandfather's nicknames (Sue and
Anthony) and St. Anne ... My grandfather is also the only Assundo
I've ever heard of. When we were in Italy we asked around and no
one there had even heard of the name either."[55]

Auxilio

Pronunciation: \ òg-ˈzi-lē-ō, aùk-ˈzi-lē-ō \

Meaning "help," Auxilio is a masculine name in Portuguese and a feminine name in Spanish. It refers to the Marian title *Maria Auxiliadora*
("Mary the Helper," also known as Our Lady, Help of Christians).

Nicknames: Zilio, Zio
Feast day: May 24 (Our Lady, Help of Christians)
See also: Auxilio (g), Perpetua (g), Socorro (g)

B

Banneux

Pronunciation: \ ˈbä-nü \

Our Lady appeared eight times in Banneux, Belgium, between January 15 and March 2, 1933. When the visionary, Mariette, asked the Lady who she was, Mary replied, "I am the Virgin of the Poor." There is a large shrine in Banneux dedicated to Our Lady today.

Though Banneux is certainly an unusual choice for a given name, and perhaps a difficult first-name choice because of its French pronunciation, in my opinion it would make a great middle name. As a first name, the nickname possibilities can make it more doable.

Nicknames: Ban, Banny, Beau, Ben, Benny

Feast day: January 15 (Our Lady of Banneux)

See also: Akita (g), Beauraing, Fatima (g), Guadalupe, Guadalupe (g), Kibeho, Kibeho (g), Knock, Lourdes, Salette (g), Tepeyac, Virginia (g), Walsingham

Bartolo

Pronunciation: \ bär-ˈtō-lō \

Blessed Bartolo Longo had been ordained a satanic priest in his post-college young adulthood before coming back to the Catholic faith of his upbringing and becoming a Third Order Dominican (religious name: Brother Rosario).

After traveling to Pompeii and seeing the sad state of the faith there, he devoted himself to the people of that city and wanted to both restore a local church and establish the Confraternity of the Rosary in order to preach the faith through the Rosary. Confraternities were then required to have an image of Our Lady giving the Rosary to St. Dominic, which Blessed Bartolo was able to acquire — a painting that included St. Rose of Lima as well as St. Dominic and Our Lady — but as it was in bad condition, Blessed Bartolo had it redone, and replaced St. Rose with St. Catherine of Siena.

The resulting image, known today as Our Lady of Pompeii or Our Lady of the Rosary, was the very image a young girl named Fortuna Agrelli said she saw in a vision of Our Lady at the end of a novena being prayed for Fortuna's healing from a variety of ill-nesses; this occurred nearly ten years after Blessed Bartolo first acquired the painting and began to restore it. Fortuna was healed, and her story inspired Pope Leo XIII to promote the Rosary even more, and he "began to write an encyclical on the Rosary almost every year … Today, the church restored by Blessed Bartolo Longo has been declared a basilica and officially designated as the Pontifical Shrine of Our Lady of the Rosary of Pompeii. It receives millions of pilgrims each year. Blessed Bartolo Longo has gained the honor of being one of the greatest champions of the Rosary in the history of the Church."[56] Indeed, in St. John Paul II's *Rosarium Virginis Mariae* (*The Rosary of the Virgin Mary*), he called Blessed Bartolo Longo "the apostle of the rosary."[57]

Nicknames: Barry, Bart, Bate, Bates, Batt, Batten, Tolly

Variants: Bartek (Polish), Bartel (Dutch), Barthélémy (French), Bartholomäus (German), Bartholomew (English), Bartlett (English), Bartolomé (Spanish), Bartosz (Polish)

Feast days: October 7 (Our Lady of the Rosary)
October 5 (Blessed Bartolo Longo)

See also: Rosario, Rosary (g), Victor, Victoria (g)

Beauraing

Pronunciation: \ ˈbō-rāŋ \

Our Lady appeared more than 30 times between November 19, 1932 and January 3, 1933 to five children (ages nine to 15) in Beauraing, Belgium. Over the course of her apparitions, Our Lady referred to herself as the Immaculate Virgin; Mother of God, Queen of Heaven; and Virgin with a Golden Heart (her heart appeared as gold during some of her visits).

Though Beauraing is an unusual choice for a given name, its similarity to the male names Beau (which can also be its nickname) and Beauregard make this a feasible choice for either a first or middle name in my opinion.

Nicknames: Beau, Bo

Feast day: August 22 (Our Lady of Beauraing)

See also: Akita (g), Aurea (g), Banneux, Caeli (g), Candace, Celeste, Celestine (b), Cora (g), Fatima (g), Guadalupe, Guadalupe (g), Immaculata (g), Kibeho, Kibeho (g), Knock, Lourdes (g), Marigold (g), Regina (g), Reginald, Reina (g), Salette (g), Tepeyac, Theotokos, Virginia (g), Walsingham

Benedict

Pronunciation: \ ˈbe-nə-dikt \

From Latin *benedicere* meaning "to speak well of, to bless," Mary is called *benedicta* in the Latin form of the Hail Mary. Additionally, Fr. Calloway called Pope Emeritus Benedict XVI "The Theologian of

the Rosary" in his book *Champions of the Rosary*, and shared about his Marian devotion:

> The Marian devotion of Pope Benedict XVI is deeply rooted in a biblical, liturgical, and ecclesial approach ... The Marian dimension of the Church is where Pope Benedict XVI's devotion to Mary has shone most plainly. He depicts the Church as a Marian mystery and shows that Our Lady has an absolutely necessary role in carrying out the providential plan of God in Christ ... He taught that if the Church were to fall silent in her praise and devotion to Mary, the Church itself would no longer be capable of glorifying God as she ought, since the Bible itself teaches the praises of Mary.[58]

Nicknames: Beck, Bede, Ben, Benny, Boon(e), Ned, Nick, Nicky

Variants: Bence (Hungarian), Ben(d)t (Danish), Benedetto (Italian), Benedikt (various), Benedykt (Polish), Benito (Italian, Spanish), Bennett (English), Benoit (French), Bento (Portuguese), Bettino (Italian)

Feast days: March 25 (Annunciation)
July 11 (St. Benedict of Nursia)

See also: Beata (g), Beatrix (g), Benedicta (g),
Gwenfair (g), Mairwen (g)

Blue

Pronunciation: \ blü \

The color blue has long been associated with Our Lady. In her apparitions she's often wearing blue (e.g., at Guadalupe she wore a blue mantle, at Lourdes she had on a blue sash); "The Blue Madonna" is

a beautiful painting by Carlo Dolci (17th century); and Ven. Fulton Sheen popularized the poem "Lovely Lady Dressed in Blue" by Mary Dixon Thayer. Boys might also like knowing about the Blue Army, founded in 1946 by Msgr. Harold J. Colgan, "as a way of helping others to live out the message of Fatima. He deliberately chose the color blue since it is often associated with Our Lady, and it was the 'blue' of Our Lady that would overcome the 'red' of Communism and Satan. The Blue Army is now known as the World Apostolate of Fatima."[59]

Feast days: February 11 (Our Lady of Lourdes)
May 13 (Our Lady of Fátima)
December 12 (Our Lady of Guadalupe)

See also: Blue (g), Fatima (g), Guadalupe, Guadalupe (g), Lourdes (g), Madonna (g), Mantle, Veil (b)

Blue in real life, literature, and/or culture

Several celebrities have included Blue in their sons' names, including actress Maria Bello, who named her son Jackson Blue, and Dylan Lauren, daughter of designer Ralph Lauren, who named her son Cooper Blue. It's definitely a unique way to add a Marian element to a boy's name.

Campion

Pronunciation: \ ˈkam-pē-ən \

The rose campion flower (*Lychnis coronaria*) was known medievally as Our Lady's Rose, and is still called Mary's Rose in parts of Europe. In Spain and Portugal it's called *Candelaria*, which is Spanish for "Candlemas," the feast that commemorates the Presentation of the Baby Jesus in the Temple (Fourth Joyful Mystery of the Rosary) and the post-birth purification of Our Lady, which is also recalled in the name for the white campion (*Silene alba*) in France: *La Chandelle de Notre Dame* ("The Candle of Our Lady"). While St. Edmund Campion's last name didn't refer to flowers or to Our Lady, the fact that he was a man, and that his surname means "champion," makes this name particularly usable for a boy.

Nicknames: Cam, Camp

Feast days: February 2 (Candlemas, also known as the Feast of the Presentation of the Baby Jesus in the Temple, as well as the Feast of the Purification of Mary) December 1 (St. Edmund Campion)

See also: Candelaria (g), Candelario, Purificación (g), Rose (g)

Candelario

Pronunciation: \ kän-də-ˈlä-ryō, kan-də-ˈler-ē-ō \

This is the masculine form of the feminine name Candelaria, which is Spanish for Candlemas, the feast that commemorates the Presentation of the Baby Jesus in the Temple (Fourth Joyful Mystery of the Rosary) and the post-birth purification of Our Lady.

Nicknames: Cande, Del, Lario, Larry, Rio

Feast Day: February 2 (Candlemas, also known as the Feast of the Presentation of the Baby Jesus in the Temple, as well as the Feast of the Purification of Mary)

See also: Candelaria (g), Purificación (g)

Cap

Pronunciation: \ ˈkap \

Cap is French for "cape," and refers to Our Lady of the Cape (*Notre Dame du Cap*), which is the name of Canada's national shrine to Our Lady. Our Lady of the Cape is also known as Our Lady of the Holy Rosary, because of the special part the Rosary played in its history — the Confraternity of the Rosary was established there in 1694, and devotion to the Rosary was reintroduced there nearly 200 years later, after having lapsed. This renewed devotion led to an increase in parishioners of the small church, and a larger one began to be built. However, a mild winter meant supplies couldn't be carried across the river as planned, so the people prayed the Rosary and, between natural occurrences and the hard work of the priest and some parishioners, a narrow ice bridge was formed and lasted long enough for the materials to be brought across (and earned the name "the Rosary bridge").

Additionally, a statue of Our Lady that had been donated by a parishioner was seen by two priests and a parishioner to open her eyes; the statue is also known as Our Lady of the Cape.[60]

I've seen Cap used as nickname for names like Casper, Caspian, Capistran, and Charles, so I think using it as is to honor Our Lady isn't unreasonable.

Nickname: Cappy

Feast day: June 23 (Our Lady of the Cape)

See also: Paderau (g), Paderau, Paidrín (g), Rosario, Rosary (g)

***Cap* in real life, literature, and/or culture**

Cap Garland was the name of a character in Laura Ingalls Wilder's *Little House on the Prairie* novels *The Long Winter*, *Little Town on the Prairie*, and *These Happy Golden Years*. He was a friend of Laura's and later one of her suitors.

Carmelo

Pronunciation: \ kär-ˈmel-ō \

Like Candelario, Carmelo is the (Spanish and Italian) masculine form of the feminine name Carmel, which refers to Our Lady of Mount Carmel.

Nicknames: Carm, Melo

Variants: Carmine (Italian), Carmo (Portuguese)

Feast day: July 16 (Our Lady of Mount Carmel)

See also: Carmel (g), Elijah, Stock

Carmelo in real life, literature, and/or culture
NBA player Carmelo Anthony bears this ultra-Marian name.

Celestine

Pronunciation: \ ˈsel-es-tēn \

Celestine is from the Latin for "heavenly," which refers to Our Lady, Queen of Heaven and Altar of Heaven. It's a feminine name as well, but has been used by five popes, so its masculinity is well documented.

Variants: Caelestis, Caelestinus, Celestino (Italian, Spanish)

Feast days: March 25 (Annunciation)
August 22 (Queenship of Mary)
May 19 (Pope St. Celestine V)

See also: Araceli, Caeli (g), Candace (g), Celeste (g), Regina, Reginald (b), Reina

Celestine in real life, literature, and/or culture
During Pope Emeritus Benedict XVI's papacy, he twice visited the tomb of Pope St. Celestine V — the only previous pope to have

resigned during his tenure. After our Pope Emeritus also resigned, the significance of those visits became clear.

Clement

Pronunciation: \ ˈkle-mənt \

This is the English form of the Late Latin name Clemens, which means "merciful" or "gentle." Both *clement* (English) and *clemens* (Latin) are used as adjectives for Our Lady in the prayer and song "Hail Holy Queen" (in Latin, *Salve Regina*).

Nickname: Clem

Variants: Clemens (various), Clemente (various), Klemens (various)

Feast days: September 24 (Our Lady of Mercy or Mercies, also known as Our Lady of Ransom)
March 15 (St. Clement Mary Hofbauer)

See also: Clementine (g), Mercy (g), Mercedes (g), Mercer, Misericordia (g), Ransom

Clement in real life, literature, and/or culture
Several popes have chosen the name Clement, as did St. Clement Mary Hofbauer (born Hansl Dvorák), the patron of my home parish.

Cruz

Pronunciations: \ ˈkrüs (Spanish — Latin America), ˈkrüth (Spanish — Spain), ˈkrüz (English) \

This Spanish word for "cross" is used for both boys and girls, and in a Marian sense refers to Our Lady at the foot of the Cross.

Variant: Croix (French)

Feast day: March 31 (Our Lady of the Holy Cross)

See also: Addolorata (g), Angustias (g), Cruz (g), Dolores (g), Iris (g), Ivy (g), John, Piedad (g), Pierce, Pieta (g), Simeon, Tristan

David

Pronunciation: \ ˈdā-vid \

In the Litany of Loreto, Our Lady is referred to as "Tower of David" (*Turris Davidica*), making this classic, perennially popular name a legitimate choice as a Marian boy name.

Nicknames: Dai, Dave, Davey, Davie, Davy, Daw, Dewey

Variants: Dafydd (Welsh), Dáibhí (Irish), Daveth (Cornish), Davi (Portuguese), Davide (Italian), Dawid (Polish), Taavet (Estonian), Taavi (Finnish)

Feast days: September 12 (Most Holy Name of Mary)
December 29 (King David)

See also: Iris (g)

Dominic

Pronunciation: \ ˈdä-mə-nik \

Saint Dominic de Guzman was the founder of the Dominican Order, and it is he who gives his name its Marian character:

Saint Dominic was a Marian saint who, as he walked from town to town preaching the Gospel, raised his voice in song

to Our Lady by preaching her Psalter and singing the *Ave Maris Stella* (Hail, Star of the Sea). His early biographers mention that he frequently received visions of the Virgin Mary and preached about her with great fervor. In one particular vision, Jesus himself informed St. Dominic that the Dominicans were entrusted to the protection of Mary ... His love for Mary is further evidenced by the fact that the primitive Constitutions of the Order required all the members to profess obedience to both God *and* the Virgin Mary.[61]

Dominican tradition holds that St. Dominic received the Rosary from Our Lady, which is depicted in the various images of Our Lady of the Rosary and explained more fully in Fr. Calloway's book *Champions of the Rosary*; St. Dominic is also credited with founding the Confraternity of the Rosary, and until 1964, only Dominican priests were allowed to bless rosaries.

Nicknames: Dimick, Dom, Dommy, Nic, Nick, Nicky, Nico

Variants: Domen (Slovak), Domenico (Italian), Dominick, Domingo (Spanish), Txomin (Basque)

Feast days: October 7 (Our Lady of the Rosary)
August 8 (St. Dominic de Guzman)

See also: Ave (g), Dimanche (g), Maris (g), Paderau, Paderau (g), Paidrín, Rosario, Rosary (g), Stella (g)

Dowson

Pronunciation: \ ˈdaů-sən \

According to Withycombe, this intriguing name is more common as a surname, and arose in the Middle Ages from the feminine first name

Dulcie, which comes from the Latin *dulcis*, meaning "sweet."[62] In the *Salve Regina* Our Lady is referred to as *dulcis*, and her name is referred to as "the sweet name of Mary" in St. Alphonsus Liguori's The *Glories of Mary*,[63] which accounts for this name being included in this volume. Dowson's similarity to the more familiar Dawson makes it seem really usable as a first name.

Nicknames: Dow, Dowse

Variants: Dowse, Dowsett, Dowsing

Feast day: September 12 (Most Holy Name of Mary)

See also: Dulcie (g)

Evett

Pronunciation: \ ˈev-ət \

With its similarity to names like Evan and Everett, I thought the surname Evett made a great addition to this volume, as it originated as a diminutive of the feminine given name Eve, which, as was discussed in the "Names for girls" section, is Marian by virtue of the fact that Our Lady is the New Eve.

Variants: Evatt, Evatts, Evetts, Evitt, Evitts
Feast day: September 12 (Most Holy Name of Mary)
See also: Eve (g)

Elijah

Pronunciation: \ i-ˈlī-jə \

In the Old Testament book of First Kings, the prophet Elijah instructed his servant to look out to the sea from Mount Carmel and report what he saw there; six times the servant reported there was nothing to see, and Elijah sent him to look again. On the seventh time, the servant told Elijah, "There is a cloud as small as a man's hand rising from the sea" (1 Kings 18:44). Carmelite tradition holds that Elijah understood this cloud to be a symbol of the Virgin Mother who would bear the Messiah, as foretold in the book of Isaiah: "Therefore the Lord himself

will give you a sign; the young woman, pregnant and about to bear a son, shall name him Emmanuel" (Is 7:14).

Carmelite tradition also suggests that this revelation of the Mother of the Messiah inspired Elijah to institute the first hermit community on Mount Carmel — the idea that he and the first Carmelite hermits loved Mary before they knew her is so moving![64]

Nickname: Eli

Variants: Elias (various), Eliot and Ellio(t)t (medieval English diminutives of Elias), Elis (various), Ellis (English), Ilia (various)

Feast days: July 16 (Our Lady of Mount Carmel)
July 20 (Elijah the Prophet)

See also: Carmel (g), Carmelo, Stock

F

Faver

Pronunciation: \ ˈfā-vər \

According to *A Dictionary of English Surnames*, Faver is a variant of the word "favor," and its meaning is given as "help, mercy, beauty" — such an incredibly Marian trio!

Nickname: Fave

Variant: Favers

Feast days: June 27 (Our Lady of Perpetual Help)
September 24 (Our Lady of Mercy or Mercies,
also known as Our Lady of Ransom)

See also: Auxilio, Auxilio (g), Gwenfair (g), Mairwen (g), Mercedes(g), Mercer, Mercy (g), Misericordia (g), Perpetua (g), Soccorro (g), Ransom

Francis, Francisco

Pronunciation: \ ˈfran-səs (Francis: English), fran-ˈsis-kō (Francisco: English), frän-ˈsēs-kō (Francisco: Spanish — Latin America), frän-ˈthēs-kō (Francisco: Spanish — Spain) \

Servant of God Francis Michael "Frank" Duff was an Irishman who started the Legion of Mary in 1921, an organization founded to bring souls to Jesus through Mary through prayer and apostolic works.

Fr. Calloway writes:

> It would prove to be an extremely fruitful Marian aposto-
> late during the 20th century, with members in almost every
> diocese in the world. Blessed Pope Paul VI described the
> Legion of Mary as the greatest movement to help souls since
> the establishment of the great mendicant religious orders in
> the 16th century! It was so effective at bringing about con-
> versions to Christ and spread so quickly to every part of the
> globe that Mao Tse-tung, the Communist leader and father
> of the People's Republic of China, referred to the Legion of
> Mary as "Public Enemy Number One."[65]

Francisco is the Spanish and Portuguese form of Francis, and was
the name of St. Francisco Marto, one of the three children to whom
Our Lady appeared in Fátima, Portugal, in 1917.

Nicknames: Chico, Curro, Fran, Frank, Frankie,
Paco, Pancho, Paquito

Variants: Francesco (Italian), Franciszek (Polish), Franco (Italian),
Frank (various), Franz (German), Patxi (Basque),
Proinsias (Irish)

Feast days: May 13 (Our Lady of Fátima)
February 20 (St. Francisco Marto)

See also: Fatima (g)

Fulton

Pronunciation: \ ˈfül-tən \

Venerable Fulton Sheen inspired this entry. He was deeply devoted to Our Lady, frequently focusing on her in his homilies and giving conferences about Mary's place in one's spiritual life, and choosing the phrase *Da per matrem me venire* ("That I may come to you through the Mother") as his motto when he became bishop. His book *The World's First Love: Mary, Mother of God* has been described as a "Marian masterpiece."[66]

Nicknames: Fil, Finn, Flash (for something like Fulton Sebastian), Flint, Flip, Fly, Flynn, Fox (for something like Fulton Xavier), Fuller, Fully, Fult, Fultie, Fulty, Fultz, Lot, Notty, Tony, Tully

Feast day: January 1 (Mary, Mother of God)

Gabriel

Pronunciation: \ ˈgā-brē-əl (English), gä-brē-ˈel (French, Spanish) \

Gabriel is a Hebrew name whose meaning is debated but variously given as "God is my strength," "strong man of God," "hero of God," or "God is my strong man," and is the name of the angel who appeared to Mary and told her that she'd been chosen by God to conceive and bear His Son. This occurrence is known as the Annunciation (meaning, the "announcement"), and is the First Joyful Mystery of the Rosary.

Nicknames: Gabe, Gib, Gil

Variants: Gábor (Hungarian), Gabriele (Italian), Gavriil (Greek, Russian), Gavril (various)

Feast days: March 25 (Annunciation)
September 29 (Feast of St. Michael,
St. Gabriel, and St. Raphael, Archangels)

See also: Annunziata (g), Fiat (g), Gabriela (g), Nunzio

Gabriel in real life, literature, and/or culture
Irish actor Gabriel Byrne (*Little Women*) is one famous bearer, and another is Ireland's TV personality Gay Byrne whose given name is the incredible Gabriel Mary Byrne. Gabriel and Mary in one boy's name? Love, love, love!

Gianmaria

Pronunciation: \ jän-mä-ˈrē-ä \

This traditional Italian male name is beautifully and explicitly Marian, combining John (Gianni) and Mary (Maria) into one name.

Nicknames: Gian, Gianni

Variant: Jean-Marie (French)

Feast days: September 12 (Most Holy Name of Mary)
December 27 (St. John the Evangelist)

See also: John, John Paul, Juan Diego

Gilmore

Pronunciation: \ ˈgil-mȯr \

The name Gilmore is an anglicization of the old Irish given name *Gillamhuire*, which literally means "servant of the Virgin Mary." From that name came the surnames Gilmore and Gilmary, as well as those deriving from *Mac Giolla Mhuire* (*Mac Gille Mhoire* in Scottish Gaelic), meaning "descendant of the servant of the Virgin Mary": MacElmurry, Kilmurry, and Kilmary.

Nicknames: Gil, Morey

Variants: Gilmary, Gilmour, Kilmary, Kilmurray, Kilmurry

Feast day: September 12 (Most Holy Name of Mary)

See also: Miles, Murray

***Gilmore* in real life, literature, and/or culture**
The name Gilmore is likely too linked to the TV show "Gilmore Girls" for many current parents, but the meaning of the name is so amazing that I hope some would be willing to reclaim it. Its friendly nicknames provide an easy way to work around the association with the show.

Gratian

Pronunciation: \ ˈgrā-sh(ē-)ən \

Gratian is essentially the male version of the name Grace, as it comes from the Latin *gratus*, meaning "grace," making it a perfect moniker for a boy to honor Our Lady of Grace. There is also a St. Gratian, who was a Roman soldier martyred for the faith in the third century.

Nickname: Gray

Variant: Graciano (Spanish, Portuguese)

Feast days: May 31 (Our Lady of Grace)
June 1 (St. Gratian of Perugia)

See also: Altagracia (g), Charity (g), Faith (g), Grace (g), Hope (g)

Guadalupe

Pronunciation: \ gwä-də-ˈlü-pä, ˈgwä-də-ˌlüp \

Guadalupe is from the Marian title Our Lady of Guadalupe, referring to an apparition by Our Lady to St. Juan Diego Cuauhtlatoatzin in Guadalupe, Mexico in the 16th century. Though commonly used as a girl's name, Guadalupe is also used as a man's name in Spanish-speaking locales.

Nickname: Lupe

Feast day: December 12 (Our Lady of Guadalupe)

See also: Akita (g), Banneux, Beauraing, Fatima (g), Guadalupe (g), Juan Diego, Kibeho, Kibeho (g), Knock, Lourdes (g), Rose (g), Salette (g), Tepeyac, Tilma (g), Walsingham

Hawthorn

Pronunciation: \ ˈhȯ-ˌthȯrn \

Our Lady has two titles that translate as "Our Lady of the Hawthorn": *Notre Dame de l'Aubépine* and *Notre Dame d'Aránzazu*, where *aubépine* and *aranza* are French and Basque, respectively, for "hawthorn." I've seen Hawthorn and Hawthorne used as first names for boys, and I think they'd make a handsome, unusual homage to Our Lady.

Nicknames: Hawk, Thorn, Thorne

Variant: Hawthorne

Feast day: June 11 (Our Lady of Aránzazu, also known as Notre Dame de l'Aubépine and Notre Dame d'Aránzazu)

See also: Ainhoa (g), Aranza (g)

***Hawthorn(e)* in real life, literature, and/or culture**
Mother Mary Alphonsa, OP, born Rose Hawthorne, was the daughter of author Nathaniel Hawthorne (perhaps most well-known for his 1850 novel *The Scarlet Letter*) and founder of the Dominican Sisters for the Care of Incurable Cancer, now known as the Dominican Sisters of Hawthorne. Her cause for canonization is currently open.

I

Iker

Pronunciation: \ ˈē-ker \

What a discovery it was to find that this intriguing Basque name meaning "visitation" is used as the Basque male form of the Spanish name Visitación, referring to the Visitation of Our Lady to her cousin Elizabeth (Second Joyful Mystery of the Rosary)!

Feast day: May 31 (Visitation of the Blessed Virgin Mary)

See also: Elizabeth (g), Visitación (g)

Iker in real life, literature, and/or culture
Soccer fans will be familiar with this name because of Spanish footballer Iker Casillas (full name Iker Casillas Fernández), known as the best goalkeeper in the history of Spanish football (soccer is called "football" in much of the world).[67]

Ivory

Pronunciation: \ ˈīv-rē, ˈī-və-rē \

"Tower of ivory" (*Turris eburnea*) is one of the titles of Our Lady included in the Litany of Loreto. According to the SSA, the name Ivory has regularly been among the top 1,000 names for both boys and girls in the U.S. since 1900.

Nicknames: Ivo, Rio

Feast days: October 16 (Purity of the Blessed Virgin Mary)
December 8 (Immaculate Conception)

See also: Biancamaria (g), Gwenfair (g), Immaculata (g),
Ivory (g), Mairwen (g), Pureza (g)

Joachim

Pronunciation: \ ˈjō-ə-kim (English), zhō-ə-ˈkēm (French),
yō-ˈä-kim (German), yō-ˈä-kēm (Polish)

If I were looking to honor a special woman with the name of my son, I might look to the men in her life for name inspiration. One of my boys has one of my maternal grandfather's names, as a nod to my mom; similarly, the father of Our Lady — grandfather of Jesus himself — would be a good person to look to for a name that calls his daughter to mind. Catholic tradition holds Joachim to be the name of Our Lady's father, husband of St. Anne. Though the name has good use across Europe, in Spanish families (in its variant Joaquín), and with several Asian saints, it's quite rare in the U.S. — a situation I'd love to see remedied!

Nicknames: Achim, Chimo, Jake, Joe, Joey,
Ximo, Jake, Jockel

Variants: Achim (German), Akim (various), Gioachino
and Gioacchino (Italian), Joakim (various),
Joaquín (Spanish), Jokin (Basque), Yakim (Russian)

Feast days: December 8 (Immaculate Conception)
July 26 (St. Joachim)
September 8 (Birth of Our Lady)

See also: Anna (g)

Joachim in real life, literature, and/or culture

Americans are most familiar with the Spanish form of Joachim, Joaquín, as it's the name of actor Joaquín Phoenix. The variant with the second-most familiarity is likely Joakim, as in NBA player Joakim Noah. The name is actually well represented in sports the world over, including retired German footballer and current manager of the German national team Joachim Löw, retired Irish hurler Joachim Kelly, and Swedish hockey players Joachim Nermark, Joachim Rohdin, and Joakim Lindström. Prince Joachim of Denmark is another notable current bearer.

There are also several Asian saints with the name, including St. Joakim Hao Kaizhi, St. Joachim Sakakibara, and St. Joaquín Royo Pérez.

John

Pronunciation: \ ˈjän \

Though John's associations are so varied that it's hard to have an overriding one, a good argument can be made for the name having a distinct Marian character in the person of Jesus' Beloved Disciple, traditionally identified as St. John the Evangelist:

> Standing by the cross of Jesus were his mother and his mother's sister, Mary the wife of Clopas, and Mary of Magdala. When Jesus saw his mother and the disciple there whom he loved, he said to his mother, "Woman, behold,

your son." Then he said to the disciple, "Behold, your mother." And from that hour the disciple took her into his home. (Jn 19:25-27)

Additionally, St. John was with Our Lady during her apparition at Knock, County Mayo, Ireland in August 1879.

Nicknames: Jack, Jake, Jay, Johnny

Variants: Eoin (Irish, Scottish), Evan (Welsh, English), Gian, Gianni (Italian), Giovanni (Italian), Hans (various), Ian (Scottish), Ivan (Russian), Jan (various), Jannick (German, Dutch), Jean (French), Jens (various), Johan (various), Jon (English), Juan (Spanish), Sean (Irish), Shane (Irish), Shawn (Irish)

Feast days: January 1 (Mary, Mother of God)
August 21 (Our Lady of Knock)
December 27 (Feast of St. John the Evangelist)

See also: Gianmaria, John Paul, Juan Diego, Knock

John Paul

Pronunciation: \ ˈjän ˈpȯl \

I debated whether or not to include John Paul as a variant of John, and decided it needed its own entry because it points very specifically to the deep Marian devotion of one man: Pope St. John Paul the Great. His motto was *Totus Tuus* ("totally yours"), which comes from St. Louis de Montfort's Marian consecration (*Totus Tuus ego sum, et omnia tua sunt. Accipio te in mea omnia. Praebe mihi cor tuum, Maria*: "I am all yours, and all that I have is yours. I take you for my all. Mary, give me your heart").[68]

His papal coat of arms contained the Cross and a letter "M" for Our Lady, and he had a great devotion to Our Lady of Fátima, as he believed she saved his life when he was shot on May 13, 1981. He wrote extensively on Marian themes as pope, including *Redemptoris Mater (On the Blessed Virgin Mary in the Life of the Pilgrim Church*, March 25, 1987), *Mulieris Dignitatem (On the Dignity of Women,* August 15, 1988), and *Rosarium Virginis Mariae (On the Most Holy Rosary*, Oct. 16, 2002), and he declared a Year of Mary (1987) and a Year of the Holy Rosary (2002) during his papacy.

Nicknames: Lolek (the nickname St. John Paul went by as a boy, a Polish diminutive of his pre-papal name, Karol), Jack, Jake, Jay, John, Johnny, John Paulie, JP

Variants: Gian Paolo (Italian), Jean-Paul (French), Johnpaul, John-Paul, Juan Pablo (Spanish)

Feast days: May 13 (Our Lady of Fátima)
October 22 (St. John Paul the Great)

See also: Clement, Clementine (g), Fatima (g), Gianmaria, John, Louis, Montfort, Paderau, Paderau (g), Paidrín, Mercedes (g), Mercer, Mercy (g), Misericordia (g), Rosario, Rosary (g)

Josemaría

Pronunciation: \ hō-sā-mä-ˈrē-ä \

This name is Marian for two reasons: first, by virtue of having "Maria" in the name itself; secondly, because of St. Josemaría Escrivá. Regarding the former, how wonderful for a boy to have both the names of St. Joseph and Our Lady in one masculine name! Regarding the latter, St. Josemaría had a great devotion to Our Lady from the time of his miraculous recovery from a life-threatening illness as a boy

after his mother pleaded to Our Lady for his healing. He frequently visited the shrine of Our Lady of the Pillar (*Nuestra Señora del Pilar*) as a seminarian, and also celebrated his first Mass there. He made many pilgrimages to Marian shrines all over Europe and Mexico City, including one to the Holy House of Loreto, where he entrusted the order he founded, Opus Dei, completely to Our Lady.

Nicknames: Pepe, Pepito (Spanish); Zé, Zezé (Portuguese)

Feast days: October 12 (Our Lady of the Pillar)
December 10 (Our Lady of Loreto)
June 26 (St. Josemaría Escrivá)

See also: Joseph, Loreto, Loretta (g), Pilar (g)

Joseph

Pronunciation: \ ˈjō-səf, ˈjō-zəf \

Like with Joachim, this is another example of looking at the male relatives of Our Lady for name inspiration. Good St. Joseph was her husband and foster father to her Son, totally committed to the woman, blessed among women, whom God asked him to marry.

Nicknames: Jody, Joe, Joey, Sepp, Seppel, Zef

Variants: Giuseppe (Italian), José (Spanish), Josef (various), Józef (Slovak, Dutch), Seosamh (Irish)

Feast days: January 1 (Mary, Mother of God)
March 19 (Feast of St. Joseph, husband of the Blessed

Virgin Mary, distinct from his feast of St. Joseph the Worker on May 1)

See also: Joachim

Juan Diego

Pronunciation: \ ˈ(h)wän dē-ˈā-gō \

Juan is the Spanish form of John, and Diego generally translates as James, yet Juan Diego together is a particularly Marian combination, as it's the name of the man to whom Our Lady appeared in Guadalupe, Mexico in 1531. During her last visit, she left her image on his *tilma* (the rough, woven garment he wore), which remains in good condition and can be seen at the Basilica of Our Lady of Guadalupe in Mexico City.

Nicknames: JD, John, Johnny, Juan, Juanito
Variant: John Diego

Feast days: December 12 (Feast of Our Lady of Guadalupe)
December 9 (Feast of St. Juan Diego Cuauhtlatoatzin)

See also: Guadalupe, Guadalupe (g), John, Rose (g), Tepeyac, Tilma (g)

Juniper

Pronunciation: \ ˈjü-nə-pər \

The juniper tree (*Juniperis*) has been known as The Madonna's Juniper Bush because, according to pious tradition, it sheltered the Holy

Family during their flight into Egypt, thus hiding them and protecting them from Herod's men. Saint Junípero Serra was a Spanish Franciscan priest who founded missions in California in the eighteenth century; Pope Francis canonized him on September 23, 2015 during his trip to the U.S.

Nicknames: Jay, Juni

Variant: Junípero (Spanish)

Feast days: January 1 (Mary, Mother of God)
July 1 (St. Junípero Serra)

See also: Juniper (g), Madonna (g), Rosemary (g)

Kibeho

Pronunciation: \ ki-ˈbā-hō \

Our Lady appeared to several teenagers in the town of Kibeho in Rwanda, Africa from 1981–1989 with a message of repentance, fasting, and praying the Rosary, and foretold what many believe to be the Rwandan genocide of 1994.

Nicknames: Bay, Bayo, Kib, Kibbie

Feast day: November 28 (Our Lady of Kibeho)

See also: Akita (g), Amabilis, Banneux, Beauraing, Fatima (g), Guadalupe, Guadalupe (g), Kibeho (g), Knock, Lourdes (g), Salette (g), Tepeyac, Walsingham

Knock

Pronunciation: \ ˈnäk \

Knock is a place in County Mayo, Ireland (in Irish: *Cnoc Mhuire* ["Hill of Mary"]), where Our Lady appeared with St. Joseph, St. John the Evangelist, Jesus as the Lamb of God, and angels on August 21, 1879, to a group of 15 villagers. Knock as a given name is a bold choice, but its similarity in sound and feel to names like Jack, Rocco, and Knox (as one of my readers pointed out), make it doable.

Nickname: Knox

Feast day: August 21 (Our Lady of Knock)

See also: Akita (g), Banneux, Beauraing, Fatima (g), Guadalupe, Guadalupe (g), John, Joseph, Kibeho, Kibeho (g), Lourdes (g), Salette (g), Tepeyac, Walsingham

Kolbe

Pronunciation: \ ˈkōl-bē, ˈkōl-bā \

Saint Maximilian Kolbe's love for Our Lady has been described as "like that of a medieval knight for his fair lady." Through his Militia of the Immaculata, he encouraged total consecration to Our Lady (similar to St. Louis de Montfort's Total Consecration to Our Lady). He named the monastery he founded in Poland "City of the Immaculate" (also known as Marytown), and started a radio and literary apostolate that focused on Our Lady. He named his magazine *Knight of the Immaculate*, and started a mission house in Nagasaki called Garden of the Immaculate. Do you see a theme? Indeed, St. Maximilian Kolbe had a great love for Our Lady under the title of the Immaculate Conception, and referred to her as the Immaculata. He's referred to in Fr. Calloway's book *Champions of the Rosary* as "The Knight of the Rosary."[69]

Nickname: Kole

Feast days: December 8 (Immaculate Conception)
August 14 (St. Maximilian Kolbe)

See also: Concepción (g), Immaculata (g), Maximilian

Leeson

Pronunciation: \ ˈlē-sən \

I'm fascinated by the surnames that have a connection to Our Lady, and Leeson is another such. It derives ultimately from the Latin *laetitia*, meaning "joy," by way of the common medieval female variant of it, Lettice, and its short form, Lece. Laetitia, Lettice, and all its variants are connected to Our Lady through her title *Causa Nostrae Laetitiae* ("Cause of Our Joy").

Nickname: Lee

Variants: Leason, Leceson, Lesson, Lisson

Feast day: December 2 (Our Lady of Joy, also known as Our Lady of Liesse)

See also: Beatrix (g), Laetitia (g), Liesse (g), Maeve (g)

Leo

Pronunciation: \ ˈlē-ō \

Leo gets its Marian character from Pope Leo XIII, who has been called "The Pope of the Rosary" — he showed his love for Our Lady through tirelessly promoting her Rosary:

Pope Leo XIII dedicated the month of October to the rosary, granted many indulgences to the rosary, approved a comprehensive list of the indulgences attached to the rosary, affirmed Rosary Sunday, supported the construction of the Basilica of the Rosary in Lourdes, inserted the title "Queen of the Most Holy Rosary" into the Litany of Loreto, wrote a charter for the Confraternity of the Rosary, encouraged the Dominicans to promote the rosary, and supported the rosary apostolate of Bl. Bartolo Longo at the Basilica of the Rosary in Pompeii. Even a shortened version of his famous Prayer to St. Michael the Archangel is now commonly prayed at the end of the rosary. The writings of Pope Leo XIII highlighted a special blessing: To pray the rosary is to pray with the holy angels, since it was the Archangel Gabriel who uttered the first Ave. Pope Leo XIII will forever be the pope of the rosary.[70]

Nickname: Lee

Variants: Leon (various), Lev (Russian), Levan (Georgian), Lew (Polish), Lionel (French)

Feast day: October 7 (Our Lady of the Rosary)

See also: Ave (g), Bartolo, Candace (g), Gabriel, Gabriela (g), Paderau, Paderau (g), Paidrín (g), Regina (g), Reginald, Reina (g), Rosario, Rosary (g)

Loreto

Pronunciation: \ lə-ˈre-tō \

Loreto is used for both boys and girls, and refers to the small town in Italy where stands the house held by tradition to be the house

in which Our Lady was born and grew up, and in which the Annunciation and the Incarnation took place (known as the Holy House of Nazareth or the Holy House of Loreto). Angels are said to have carried the house there in the 13th century. There's also a beautiful prayer in honor of Our Lady called the Litany of Loreto, which lists the Marian titles that have inspired so many of the names in this book.

Nicknames: Rett, Retto

Feast day: December 10 (Our Lady of Loreto)

See also: Annunziata (g), Loretta (g), Nazaret (g), Nazario, Nunzio

Louis

Pronunciation: \ ˈlü-is (English), ˈlü-ē (French), lü-ˈē (French) \

I included Louis because of St. Louis-Marie Grignion de Montfort, who was known for his deep devotion to Our Lady and wrote the classic Marian works *True Devotion to Mary*, *The Secret of Mary*, and *The Secret of the Rosary*. (The recent popular *33 Days to Morning Glory: A Do-It-Yourself Retreat in Preparation for Marian Consecration* by Fr. Michael Gaitley, MIC [Stockbridge, MA: Marian Press, 2011], presents a retooling of St. Louis' 33-day period of preparation leading up to a total consecration to Our Lady.)

St. Louis' writings had a significant influence on Pope St. John Paul the Great, who took his motto from St. Louis' consecration to Our Lady: *Totus Tuus* ("totally yours"). Fr. Calloway, in his book *Champions of the Rosary*, describes St. Louis as "one of the greatest Marian saints of all time, if not the greatest."[71]

Nicknames: Lou, Louie

Variant: Lewis

Feast days: September 12 (Most Holy Name of Mary)
April 28 (St. Louis-Marie Grignion de Montfort)

See also: John Paul, Montfort, Paderau, Paderau (g),
Paidrín (g), Rosario, Rosary (g)

Lucian

Pronunciation: \ ˈlü-shən \

From the Latin *lux*, meaning "light," Lucian is a perfect nod to Our
Lady of Light (*Nuestra Señora de la Luz* in Spanish).

Nicknames: Lou, Luc

Variants: Luciano (Italian, Spanish, Portuguese), Lucio (Italian,
Spanish), Lucius (English)

Feast day: February 27 (Our Lady of Light)

See also: Lux, Luz (g)

Lucius and _Luciano_ in real life, literature, and/or culture
Unfortunately, in recent years Lucius has taken on a sinister feel
for many, due to baddie Lucius Malfoy in the *Harry Potter* series.
The nicknames Luc or Lou can help hide that association, and the

variant Lucian might be the safer choice overall, or one of the other variants, like Luciano — the late great Luciano Pavarotti was a well-known Italian operatic tenor.

Luke

Pronunciation: \ lük \

Though Luke looks as though it would be related to the Luc- names (Lucian, Lucy), which have to do with light and can refer to Our Lady of Light, it's actually unrelated, referring instead to a person from the southern Italian region of Lucania. Such was the meaning behind the name of St. Luke the Evangelist, and it's he who gives this name a Marian character. The Gospel of Luke is intensely Marian, containing the accounts of the Annunciation and the Visitation; the prophecy that Our Lady's heart would be pierced by a sword; the first half of the Hail Mary; and Our Lady's beautiful canticle of praise, the Magnificat.

Nicknames: Lolek (suggested by one of my readers as a nickname for Luke that can also acknowledge St. John Paul, as it was his childhood nickname), Lou, Lucky, Lukey

Variants: Luca (various), Lucas (various), Luka (various)

Feast days: March 25 (Annunciation)
May 31 (Visitation of the Blessed Virgin Mary)
September 15 (Our Lady of Sorrows)
October 18 (St. Luke the Evangelist)

See also: Addolorata (g), Angustias (g), Annunziata (g), Ave (g), Dolores (g), Elizabeth (g), Gabriel, Gabriela (g), John Paul, Magnificat (g), Nunzio, Piedad (g), Pierce, Pieta (g), Simeon, Visitación (g), Tristan

Mantle

Pronunciation: \ ˈman-təl \

The name Mantle is most familiar as a surname, deriving from the French word meaning "coat" or "cloak." Its Marian connection comes from the fact that Our Lady always wears a mantle (also referred to as her veil), and there's a particularly beautiful story regarding her mantle and St. Dominic. He had a vision in which he saw all the religious orders of the Church in Heaven, but he couldn't see his own. This saddened him, and Our Lord asked him if he'd like to see where the Dominicans were. Of course St. Dominic said "yes," and then witnessed an amazing sight:

> Our Lord, putting his hand upon the shoulders of the Blessed Virgin, said to blessed Dominic, "I have entrusted your Order to my Mother." Then the Blessed Virgin opened the cape that covered her and spread it out before blessed Dominic. It seemed vast enough to cover the entire Heaven and, under it, he saw a large multitude of his brethren.[72]

Our Lady's cape, under which the Dominican Order sheltered, is also known as her mantle. I think this name is very doable for a boy, especially considering the other famous Mantle (see the "*Mantle* in real life, literature, and/or culture" section below).

Nicknames: Manny, Manty

Feast day: September 12 (Most Holy Name of Mary)

See also: Blue, Blue (g), Dominic, Veil (g)

***Mantle* in real life, literature, and/or culture**
The name Mantle would most likely call baseball legend Mickey Mantle to mind for most people, which makes it a really fun name for a Catholic boy — totally Marian, and easy to "wear" because of other positive, masculine associations.

Maria, Marie

See Mary.

Mariano, Mario

Pronunciation: \ mer-ē-ˈä-no (Mariano); ˈmä-ryō, ˈmä-rē-ō (Mario) \

Neither Mariano nor Mario are etymologically related to the name Mary, being instead forms of Marius, which may be derived either from the Roman god of war (Mars) or from the Latin *mas, maris* meaning "male." But as several sources noted, both Mariano and Mario have a long history of use as masculine forms of Maria.

Variants: Marianus (various), Marius (various)
Feast day: September 12 (Most Holy Name of Mary)

Mario **in real life, literature, and/or culture**

From "Saved by the Bell" actor Mario Lopez, to author of
The Godfather Mario Puzo, to the "Super Mario Bros." video games,
to racing legend Mario Andretti, to Pope Francis himself
(his pre-papal name was Jorge Mario Bergoglio), Mario has long
been used for boys, and is a great way to honor Our Lady.

Marriott

Pronunciation: \ ˈmer-ē-ät, ˈmer-ē-ət \

Marriott is a surname derived from Mary, via Mary's medieval diminutive Mariot. The Marriott hotel chain could be a pro (as the name is familiar) or a con (as it's the most overriding current association), but its Marian character can't be denied.

Nicknames: Mitt, Mitty, Mott, Motts, Riot (for the bold!)

Variants: Mariot, Marriot

Feast day: September 12 (Most Holy Name of Mary)

Mary

Pronunciation: \ ˈmer-ē, ˈma-rē, ˈmā-rē \

The most Marian of all names has been borne by men as well as women for centuries. Parents have given it to their sons in the first and middle spots, and priests and brothers have taken it as part of their religious name. One might say, it takes a real man to bear the name of his Mother!

Variants: Maria (various), Marian (English), Marie (French), Marion (French)

Feast day: September 12 (Most Holy Name of Mary)

See also: Gianmaria, Gilmore, Josemaría, Mariano, Mario, Marriott, Mary (g), Miles, Murray

Mary, Maria, Marie, Marian, Marion
for boys in real life, literature, and/or culture

Where to begin! There are several male saints with a form of Mary in their names, like St. Clement Mary Hofbauer, St. Louis-Marie Grignion de Montfort, St. Anthony Mary Claret, St. Maximilian Maria Kolbe, St. Josemaría Escrivá, St. John Marie Vianney, Blessed Thomas Maria Fusco, and Blessed Marian Górecki. Recently, I've seen priests and brothers of the Franciscan Missionaries of the Eternal Word (MFVA) and the Dominican Order take Mary as part of their religious names, and I'm sure there are many others. And even Hollywood has its own example: The rough, tough, manly man actor John Wayne was born Marion Robert Morrison.

Maximilian

Pronunciation: \ mak-sə-ˈmil-yən \

This name points to the greatness of Our Lady, as Maximilian means "greatest," as well as to St. Maximilian Kolbe, whose love for Our Lady, especially as the Immaculate Conception, was discussed in the entry for Kolbe.

Nicknames: Mac, Max, Miles, Milo

Variants: Maksymilian (Polish), Massimiliano (Italian), Maximiliano (Spanish, Portuguese), Maximilien (French), Maximillian (English), Miksa (Hungarian)

Feast days: December 8 (Immaculate Conception) August 14 (St. Maximilian Kolbe)

See also: Concepción (g), Immaculata (g), Kolbe

Mercer

Pronunciation: \ ˈmər-sər \

Though Mercer is a surname that derived from the occupation "trader" (*mercier* in Old French), Oxford's *Dictionary of First Names* notes that it "may sometimes also have been chosen as a kind of male equivalent of Mercy," which points to Our Lady of Mercy.[73]

Nickname: Merce

Feast day: September 24 (Our Lady of Mercy,
also known as Our Lady of Ransom)

See also: Clement, Clementine (g), Mantle, Mercedes (g),
Mercy (g), Misericordia (g), Ransom

Miles

Pronunciation: \ ˈmī(-ə)lz \

Like Gilmore, Miles is an Anglicization of an old Irish name — in this
case, *Maolmhuire*, meaning "servant of the Virgin Mary."

Variants: Maelmarius (Latin), Maolra (Irish),
Milo (English, Germanic), Myles (English)

Feast day: September 12 (Most Holy Name of Mary)

See also: Gilmore, Murray

Mitrofan

Pronunciation: \ mi-trə-ˈfan \

This intriguing name is the Russian form of the Greek *Metrophanes*,
which according to Oxford's *Dictionary of First Names* means "'appearance of the Mother' (i.e. Mary, Mother of God)."[74] An impeccably
Marian name for a boy!

Nickname: Mitya (Russian)

Variant: Metrophanes (Greek)

Feast day: January 1 (Mary, Mother of God)

See also: Madonna (g), Theotokos

Molson

Pronunciation: \ ˈmōl-sən \

This English surname, dating back to the 14th century, means "son of Moll," where Moll is a diminutive of Mary.

Nickname: Molse

Feast day: September 12 (Most Holy Name of Mary)

See also: Corona (g), Molly (g)

***Molson* in real life, literature, and/or culture**
While I think Molson does hold appeal, even if only to those interested in the Marian connections of names (rather than those who are naming babies), it's an unfortunate fact that the brand of beer with the same name will be most people's first association.

Montfort

Pronunciation: \ ˈmänt-fərt (English), mōⁿ-ˈför (French) \

Montfort is the surname of St. Louis de Montfort, whose first name is also included in this volume, by virtue of his deep devotion to Our Lady and his classic Marian works *True Devotion to Mary*, *The Secret of Mary*, and *The Secret of the Rosary*. One of my blog readers recently suggested Montfort as a first name with the nickname Monty, which I thought was brilliant.

Nickname: Monty

Feast days: September 12 (Most Holy Name of Mary)
April 28 (St. Louis-Marie Grignion de Montfort)

See also: Louis

Murray

Pronunciation: \ ˈmər-ē \

Though Murray appears to have arisen from a number of different origins, one of them is as a variant of the Irish *Mac Giolla Mhuire* — "son of the servant of Mary" — which is also anglicized as MacElmurry, Kilmary, Kilmurray, and Kilmurry.

Variant: Murry (English)

Feast day: September 12 (Most Holy Name of Mary)

See also: Gilmore, Miles

N

Nazario

Pronunciation: \ nä-ˈzä-ryō, nä-ˈtsä-ryō (Italian), nä-ˈsä-ryō
(Spanish — Latin America), nä-ˈthä-ryō (Spanish — Spain) \

Nazario means "from Nazareth," and can be considered Marian via
Our Lady's title "Our Lady of Nazareth." Not only can that title refer to
the fact that Nazareth was Mary's hometown as well as the location of
her *fiat* and the Annunciation and Incarnation, but also to a particular
statue of Our Lady and Baby Jesus that, tradition holds, was carved by
St. Joseph himself and later painted by St. Luke, and passed through
the generations by such notable figures as St. Jerome and St. Augus-
tine. It currently resides in Portugal, and there's also a great devotion
to her under this title in Brazil.

Nicknames: Rio, Zario

Variants: Nazaire (French), Nazar (Russian, Ukrainian),
Nazarius (Latin)

Feast day: March 6 (Our Lady of Nazareth)

See also: Annunziata (g), Belén (g), Fiat (g), Joseph, Luke,
Nazaret (g), Nunzio

Nunzio

Pronunciation: \ ˈnün(t)-sē-ō \

I'm always interested to find male names that are derived from female names, and Nunzio is one: The Behind the Name website says it's the masculine short form of the feminine Annunziata,[75] which refers to the Annunciation, when the Angel Gabriel announced to Our Lady that she'd been chosen by God to conceive and bear His Son (First Joyful Mystery of the Rosary).

Nicknames: Nunzi, Zio

Variant: Nuncio

Feast day: March 25 (Annunciation)

See also: Ancilla (g), Annunziata (g), Fiat (g), Gabriel, Gabriela (g)

Nuncio in real life, literature, and/or culture
A familiar variant in this family of names is the word "nuncio," which is derived from the same Latin root as annunciation: *nuntius* ("messenger" or "message"). The Holy See assigns ambassadors — called papal or apostolic nuncios — to foreign governments.

O

Oliver

Pronunciation: \ ˈä-lə-vər \

Though it appears that Oliver is not etymologically related to "olive," its appearance and sound are so similar to "olive" that it could easily be considered a Marian name via her title Our Lady of Olives, as well as Our Lady of Peace (as an olive branch is a symbol of peace).

Nicknames: Noll, Nollie, Ollie

Variant: Olivier (French)

Feast days: June 18 (Our Lady of Olives)
July 9 (Our Lady, Queen of Peace)

See also: Olivia (g), Pace, Paloma (g), Pax, Paz (g)

P

Pace

Pronunciation: \ ˈpās (English), ˈpä-chā (Italian) \

Whether in English or Italian, Pace means "peace," and is an interesting nod to Our Lady, Queen of Peace. The \ ˈpās \ pronunciation fits in neatly with the surname trend in baby names, while the Italian \ ˈpä-chā \ has a more ethnic and catacomb-like feel to it.

Variant: Pax

Feast days: July 9 (Our Lady, Queen of Peace)
November 21 (Our Lady of Peace, El Salvador)

See also: Olivia (g), Oliver, Paloma (g), Pax, Paz (g)

Paderau

Pronunciation: \ ˈpä-dā-rā, pä-ˈde-rī \

Meaning "beads" or "rosary" in Welsh, Paderau can be used for both boys and girls. With the possible nickname "Paddy" already being an established male nickname, Paderau is totally doable as an unusual Marian first or middle name for a boy.

Nicknames: Derry, Paddy, Roy, Rye

Feast day: October 7 (Our Lady of the Rosary)

See also: Bartolo, Cap, Paderau (g), Paidrín (g), Rosario, Rosary (g), Victor, Victoria (g)

Panagiotis

Pronunciation: \ pä-nä-yō-tis \

Like Nunzio, Panagiotis is a male name derived from a female name — in this case, Panagiota, a Greek title for Our Lady meaning "all holy," from *pan* meaning "all" and *hagios* meaning "holy." It's a name commonly given in Our Lady's honor.

Nicknames: Panos, Takis
Feast day: August 15 (Assumption)
See also: Panagiota (g), Santamaria (g)

Pax

Pronunciation: \ ˈpaks, ˈpäks \

Pax means "peace" in Latin, and can be bestowed in honor of Our Lady of Peace.

Variant: Pace
Feast days: July 9 (Our Lady, Queen of Peace)
November 21 (Our Lady of Peace, El Salvador)

See also: Olivia (g), Oliver, Pace, Paloma (g), Paz (g)

Peyton

Pronunciation: \ ˈpā-tən \

Venerable Fr. Patrick Peyton, referred to as "The Rosary Priest" by Fr. Calloway in his book *Champions of the Rosary*, is the inspiration behind this entry. He started the Family Rosary Crusade in the 1940s, which was an international Rosary apostolate, and "organized rosary events in more than 40 countries, gathering over 28 million people to pray the rosary" — all stemming from his love for Our Lady.[76] Fr. Calloway writes:

> While a seminarian, [Fr. Peyton] was healed from tuberculosis as a result of praying a novena to Our Lady ... During his time as a seminarian in the United States, after his healing from tuberculosis took place, his love for Mary turned into an apostolate. He understood his mission in life to be spreading devotion to Mary and her rosary, writing several books and addressing crowds across the world. Mary was his princess. He was honored to bring solid teaching about his princess to every nation, and often referred to himself as "Mary's donkey." The famous actress Loretta Young once made the remark that she had never met a man so in love with a woman as Fr. Peyton was in love with the Blessed Virgin Mary.[77]

Nicknames: Peyt, Pey

Feast day: October 7 (Our Lady of the Rosary)

See also: Paderau, Paderau (g), Paidrín (g), Rosario, Rosary (g)

Pierce

Pronunciation: \ ˈpirs \

Pierce is actually a form of Peter, meaning "rock," and therefore not etymologically related to Mary in any way. However, I know of a baby boy named Pierce after the Prophecy of Simeon, which stated that Mary's heart would be pierced by a sword (a reference to her grief at all that her Son would suffer; see Luke 2:35). What an interesting and appropriate way to name a boy for Our Lady!

Feast day: September 15 (Our Lady of Sorrows)

See also: Addolorata (g), Anna (g), Dolores (g), Iris (g), Ivy (g), Piedad (g), Pieta (g), Simeon, Tristan

Pio

Pronunciation: \ ˈpē-ō \

An Italian form of Pius (meaning "pious, devout"), Pio most often calls St. (Padre) Pio of Pietrelcina to mind, but I'm assigning it a Marian character because it's the male variant of Pia, which is used to describe Our Lady in the *Salve Regina*.

Variant: Pius (Latin)

Feast days: September 12 (Most Holy Name of Mary)
September 23 (St. Pio of Pietrelcina)

See also: Pia (g), Piedad (g), Pius

Pius

Pronunciation: \ ˈpī-əs \

Though the previous entry, Pio, is a variant of Pius, I thought Pius needed its own entry, for two reasons. The first is Pope St. Pius V, who has several Marian attributes to recommend him, including this one:

> In his zeal for standardizing the liturgy, St. Pope Pius V revised the Divine Office (Liturgy of the Hours) in 1568. As part of the revision, he inserted the complete version of the Hail Mary prayer (already in use in other breviaries) into the universal Roman Breviary. This action officially established the complete Hail Mary prayer — the exact version

we pray today — as the universally approved formula. The complete version of the Hail Mary did not originate with the pontificate of St. Pope Pius V, since it had been in use since the 14th century, but to his perpetual honor and credit, he established it as the universal norm. ... Saint Pope Pius V is buried in the greatest Marian church of the Catholic world, the Basilica of Santa Maria Maggiore in Rome.[78]

Additionally, St. Pope Pius V was the pope who asked Christendom to pray the Rosary for protection against the Muslims in the Battle of Lepanto, and before the news of the outcome reached Rome he'd already received a vision from Our Lady letting him know that the Holy League had been victorious. He then established the feast of Our Lady of Victory on October 7, which is now known as the feast of Our Lady of the Rosary. St. Louis de Montfort, himself a saint with incredible Marian credentials, called St. Pope Pius V "one of the greatest Popes who ever ruled the Church."[79]

Secondly, Pope Pius XII issued the Marian papal encyclical Ad *Caeli Reginam* (On Proclaiming the Queenship of Mary) in 1954.

Feast days: October 7 (Our Lady of the Rosary, formerly known as Our Lady of Victory) April 30 (Pope St. Pius V)

See also: Caeli (g), Candace (g), Louis, Montfort, Paderau, Paderau (g), Paidrín (g), Pio, Pia (g), Regina (g), Reina (g), Reginald, Rosario, Rosary (g), Victor, Victoria (g)

R

Ransom

Pronunciation: \ ˈran(t)-səm \

Ransom is a fun option for a boy — one hundred percent Marian with a touch of pirate! In the 13th century, Our Lady appeared separately to St. Peter Nolasco and King James I of Aragon, asking them to start an Order devoted to rescuing Christians who had been captured by Muslims. Saint Peter Nolasco's confessor, the Dominican St. Raymond of Peñafort, encouraged him and King James offered his protection, and so St. Peter started the Order of Our Lady of Ransom, now called the Order of the Blessed Virgin Mary of Mercy, or the Order of Mercy, or the Mercedarians.

The Mercedarians take the usual three vows of poverty, obedience, and chastity, and add in a fourth: to give up their own lives if needed for others whose faith is in danger. In the 13th century, that meant exchanging themselves for Christian slaves; currently, Mercedarians seek to help those whose faith is in danger because of social, political, and psychological issues by working with the imprisoned, the poor, the hospitalized, those who struggle with drug addiction, and families.

Nicknames: Ran, Rance

Feast day: September 24 (Our Lady of Ransom)

See also: Clement, Clementine (g), Mercy (g), Mercedes (g), Mercer, Misericordia (g), Remedios (g)

Refugio

Pronunciation: \ rə-ˈfü-zhyō, rə-ˈfyü-jyō \

This traditional boys' name is from the Spanish Marian title *Nuestra Señora del Refugio* ("Our Lady of Refuge," also known as Our Lady, Refuge of Sinners), which refers to both a title under which Our Lady is patroness of Baja California, Mexico and the state of California (Alta California), and to an image of Our Lady and the Baby Jesus, both crowned.

Nicknames: Gio, Ref, Reg, Reggie
Feast days: July 4 (Our Lady of Refuge, Baja California)
July 5 (Our Lady of Refuge, Alta California)
See also: Amparo (g)

Reginald

Pronunciation: \ ˈrej-i-nəld \

Reginald is from a Latinized variant of the old German name Raginald (which combines the elements *ragin* ["advice"] and *wald* ["rule"]), and its Marian character comes from the fact that its Latinized spelling was influenced by *regina* ("queen").[80] An added Marian element comes from 20th-century theologian Fr. Reginald Garrigou-LaGrange, OP, who taught St. John Paul II in his early priesthood, and was "renowned as an erudite Mariologist. He was so well respected that he was asked by Venerable Pope Pius XII to be a theological consultant as the Holy Father formulated the dogmatic declaration of the Assumption of Mary, promulgated in 1950."[81]

Nicknames: Reg, Reggie

Variants: Raghnall (Irish), Ragnvald (Swedish, Norwegian), Reinhold (German), Reynaldo (Spanish), Re(y)naud (French), Reynold (English), Ronald (Scottish)

Feast day: August 22 (Queenship of Mary)

See also: Assumpta (g), Assunto, Candace (g), Incoronata (g), John Paul, Pius, Regina (g), Reina (g), Rennison

Rennison

Pronunciation: \ ˈren-i-sən \

The old English surname Rennison is perhaps a bit of stretch, as its meaning — "son of Reynold" — is one step away from the Reynold variant Reginald, which is included in this volume by virtue of the fact that its spelling was influenced by *regina* ("queen"). But it's a popular practice to bestow last names as given names, and in keeping with my hope of providing a lot of good Marian possibilities for boys, of all styles, I thought Rennison was too cool not to include.

Nicknames: Ren, Renny

Variants: Renison, Renilson, Rennilson, Renson

Feast day: August 22 (Queenship of Mary)

See also: Regina (g), Reginald, Reina (g)

Reyes

Pronunciation: \ ˈrā-yes \

Used for both boys and girls, Reyes is a truncation of the Spanish titles *La Virgen de los Reyes* or *Nuestra Señora de los Reyes* ("The Virgin of the Kings" or "Our Lady of the Kings," respectively), which refer to a miraculous sculpture of Our Lady that was given to King Ferdinand III of Castile and León in Spain (he died in 1252). Through this statue, the king was assured by Our Lady that he would be successful in reclaiming Seville from the Muslims who occupied it, and it came to pass not long after. The statue still resides in the Cathedral of Seville above the incorrupt body of the now St. Ferdinand III.[82]

Nickname: Rey

Feast days: August 15 (Our Lady of the Kings, as well as the Assumption of Our Lady)
May 30 (St. Ferdinand III of Castile)

See also: Reyes (g)

Romero

Pronunciation: \ rō-ˈme-rō \

Romero is the Spanish word for the rosemary plant, giving it a great Marian connection, and the last name of Blessed Óscar Romero gives it a strong masculine touch.

Feast days: September 12 (Most Holy Name of Mary)
March 24 (Blessed Óscar Romero)

See also: Rosemary (g)

Rosario

Pronunciation: \ rō-ˈzär-ē-ō, rō-ˈsär-ē-ō \

Meaning "rosary," Rosario is a masculine name in Italian and feminine in Spanish. Blessed Bartolo Longo was given the name Br. Rosario when he took his vows as a Third Order Dominican.

Nicknames: Charo, Rio, Sarino, Soddy

Variants: Rosaire (French), Rosarian, Rosarium (Latin)

Feast days: October 7 (Our Lady of the Rosary)
October 5 (Blessed Bartolo Longo)

See also: Bartolo, Cap, Dominic, Paderau, Paderau (g), Paidrín (g), Prouille (g), Rosary (g), Rose (g), Victor, Victoria (g)

Rosario in real life, literature, and/or culture
The father of my mom's dear friend and college roommate, himself a first-generation Italian-American, was named Rosario and went by Soddy.

Royce

Pronunciation: \ ˈrȯis \

This traditional male name is from a medieval variant of Rose, which makes Royce an entirely appropriate way to name a little boy for Our Lady. The Rolls-Royce connection gives it an added masculine "oomph."

Nickname: Roy

Variant: Royston

Feast day: September 12 (Most Holy Name of Mary)

See also: Rose (g)

Seraphim

Pronunciation: \ ˈser-ə-fim \

The seraphim are one of the orders of angels — they are those who "stand before God as ministering servants in the heavenly court."[83] In the Bible, one of the seraphim purifies Isaiah's lips with a burning coal from Heaven, and the seraphim are also mentioned in the Book of Enoch, as well as in the Preface of the Mass. The name's Marian character comes from Our Lady's title "Queen of the Angels."

Nicknames: Finn, Phim, Serap

Variants: Serafim (various), Serafin (Polish), Serafino (Italian), Seraphin (French)

Feast day: August 2 (Our Lady of the Angels)

See also: Angela (g), Angelo, Candace (g), Regina (g), Reina (g), Reginald, Seraphina (g)

Simeon

Pronunciation: \ ˈsi-mē-ən \

The Prophecy of Simeon is the first of the Seven Sorrows of Our Lady, and it occurred during the Presentation of the Baby Jesus in the Temple (Fourth Joyful Mystery of the Rosary). The Holy Spirit had

revealed to Simeon that he wouldn't die before he'd seen the promised Messiah. When the Holy Family came into the temple, he recognized the Child, and after blessing them he told Mary, "Behold, this child is destined for the fall and rise of many in Israel, and to be a sign that will be contradicted (and you yourself a sword will pierce) so that the thoughts of many hearts may be revealed" (Lk 2:34-35).

Nickname: Sim

Variant: Simon

Feast days: February 2 (Candlemas, also known as the Feast of the Presentation of the Baby Jesus in the Temple, as well as the Feast of the Purification of Mary) September 15 (Our Lady of Sorrows)

See also: Addolorata (g), Angustias (g), Anna (g), Candelaria (g), Candelario, Dolores (g), Iris, Ivy, Piedad (g), Pierce, Pieta (g), Purificación (g), Tristan

Stock

Pronunciation: \ ˈstäk \

Saint Simon Stock was a Carmelite who had the great privilege of receiving the Brown Scapular from Our Lady in the 13th century:

> In answer to his appeal for help for his oppressed order, she appeared to him with a scapular in her hand and said: "Take, beloved son this scapular of thy order as a badge of my confraternity and for thee and all Carmelites a special sign of grace; whoever dies in this garment, will not suffer

everlasting fire. It is the sign of salvation, a safeguard in dangers, a pledge of peace and of the covenant" ... even though there is here no direct reference to the members of the scapular confraternity, indirectly the promise is extended to all who from devotion to the Mother of God should wear her habit or badge, like true Christians, until death, and be thus as it were affiliated to the Carmelite Order.[84]

Stock is a bold choice, but doable due to its similarity in sound to names like Jack, Rocco, and Knox, as well as fitting into the last-name-as-first-name trend.

Feast days: July 16 (Our Lady of Mount Carmel)
May 16 (St. Simon Stock)

See also: Carmel (g), Carmelo, Elijah

Tepeyac

Pronunciation: \ ˈtep-ä-yak \

Tepeyac (also known as the Hill of Tepeyac) is the name of the place where Our Lady of Guadalupe appeared to St. Juan Diego, and where the Basilica of Our Lady of Guadalupe (which houses St. Juan Diego's *tilma* with its miraculous image of Our Lady) currently stands. Though I've never seen Tepeyac used as a gien name, I think it has great possibility for such use, especially perhaps as a middle name.

Nicknames: Pac, Packy, Tac, Tep, Tepay, Teppy

Feast days: December 12 (Our Lady of Guadalupe)
December 9 (Feast of St. Juan Diego Cuauhtlatoatzin)

See also: Akita (g), Banneux, Beauraing, Fatima (g), Guadalupe, Guadalupe (g), Juan Diego, Kibeho, Kibeho (g), Knock, Lourdes (g), Salette (g), Tilma (g), Walsingham

Theotokos

Pronunciation: \ thē-ə-ˈtō-kōs \

Theotokos, literally meaning "God-bearer," is a title of Our Lady, referring to her role as Mother of God. As an art term, it's more commonly used in the Eastern churches and refers to a depiction of Our Lady (similar to the way *Madonna* is used in the West). As Theodore, Theobald, and even just Theo on its own are acceptable given names for

boys, I think Theotokos can fit right in and be a beautiful, reverent name in honor of Our Lady.

Nickname: Theo

Feast day: January 1 (Mary, Mother of God)

See also: Candace (g), Madonna (g), Mitrofan

Tristan

Pronunciation: \ ˈtris-tən \

Though Tristan seems to have originated as a variant of the name Drustan, which is unrelated to Our Lady in any way, the Latin word *tristis* ("sad") played a role in its evolution from Drustan to Tristan due to the old and well-known tragic story of Tristan and Isolde. Its sad connotations give the name a great connection to Our Lady of Sorrows.

Nicknames: Tris, Trip (perhaps with a P middle name)

Variants: Tristano (Italian), Tristen (English), Tristian (English), Tristin (English), Triston (English), Tristram (English), Trystan (Welsh)

Feast Day: September 15 (Feast of Our Lady of Sorrows)

See also: Addolorata (g), Angustias (g), Dolores (g), Iris (g), Ivy (g), Piedad (g), Pierce, Pieta (g), Simeon

Tristan and _Tristram_ in real life, literature, and/or culture
Not only is Tristan, Knight of the Round Table, one of the main characters in the story _Tristan and Isolde_, but it's also the name of Brad Pitt's character in the 1994 film "Legends of the Fall" (which was likely responsible for the fairly sizable bump in Tristan's popularity in the following year's name statistics). Tristan Thompson is also a current NBA player.

The variant Tristram is perhaps best known from the 18th-century novel _The Life and Opinions of Tristram Shandy, Gentleman_ (or _Tristram Shandy_) by Laurence Sterne.

Victor

Pronunciation: \ ˈvik-tər, ˈbēk-tȯr (Spanish) \

Our Lady of Victory is another name for Our Lady of the Rosary, and commemorates the victory of the Christian army against the Ottoman forces at the Battle of Lepanto in 1571, during which Pope Pius V had asked all of Europe to pray the Rosary and ask Our Lady to intercede for the Christians during the battle. The fact that Victor's Marian connection is a battle might be particularly appealing for a boy.

Nicknames: Vic, Vicho, Vick, Vico, Victo, Vio, Vito, Vitty

Feast day: October 7 (Our Lady of the Rosary)

See also: Paderau, Padera (g), Paidrín, Pius, Rosario, Rosary (g), Victoria (g)

Victor in real life, literature, and/or culture
I did a post on my blog in May 2015 in response to a reader request for nickname ideas for Victor, and as of the end of October 2017, it remains my fifth-most-viewed post of all time.

Walsingham

Pronunciation: \ ˈwäl-siŋ-əm, ˈwäl-siŋ-həm \

In the 11th century, Lady Richeldis de Faverches reported that Our Lady had appeared to her and shown her the house in Nazareth where the Annunciation had occurred, and asked her to build a replica in Walsingham, England. So it was built, and became known as "The Holy House" and "England's Nazareth," and became an important medieval shrine.[85] Though the original shrine was destroyed during the Reformation, it was refounded three centuries later, and in 2015 Pope Francis named the Shrine of Our Lady of Walsingham a Minor Basilica. Our Lady of Walsingham is patroness of England.[86]

Walsingham struck me as similar to the kinds of surnames one might consider as a first name for a boy (like Wentworth, Whitaker, and Wilder, all having current usage as first names), and the possible Walter-esque nicknames made it seem especially doable.

Nicknames: Wales, Wally, Walsy, Walt

Feast day: September 24 (Our Lady of Walsingham)

See also: Akita (g), Banneux, Beauraing, Fatima (g), Guadalupe, Guadalupe (g), Kibeho, Kibeho (g), Knock, Lourdes (g), Salette (g), Tepeyac

William

Pronunciation: \ 'wil-yəm \

This traditional boys' name is also the name of two flowers — Sweet William (*Dianthus barbatus*) and Wild Sweet William (*Phlox divaricata*) — which used to be known as Mary's Rose and Our Lady's Wedding, respectively. There are also quite a few Sts. William.

Nicknames: Bill, Billy, Liam, Wil, Wilkie, Wilkins, Will, Willie, Wills, Willy

Feast day: September 12 (Most Holy Name of Mary)

Other ideas for naming after Our Lady

I've seen parents consider some really creative ideas when seeking to name their little ones after Our Lady. For example, one of my readers named her daughter Sylvie Regina — such a brilliant soundalike to the *Salve Regina*! Another considered the initials A.V.E., as a nod to *Ave Maria*, and another considered the initials B.V.M., for the Blessed Virgin Mary. Others could include A.R.K., for Our Lady being the Ark of the New Covenant, or O.L. for Our Lady. Using initials is a nice approach for choosing a Marian boy's name as well.

There are also some gorgeous combinations and mash-ups — or *portmanteaus* — of Mary/Maria/Marie and other names that I've come across, including:

Macha (French; Marie + Charlotte)

Malou (French; Marie + Louise)

Mariale (Spanish; Maria + Alejandra)

Marianela (Spanish; Maria + Estela)

Mariassunta (Italian; Maria + Assunta)

Maricel (Spanish; Maria + Celia)

Marielise (French; Marie + Elise or Elisabeth)

Marieva (Spanish; Maria + Eva)

Marifé (Spanish; Maria + Fe)

Marlies (Dutch; Maria + Elisabeth)

Marilu (Spanish; Maria + Luisa, Luz)

Matrice (Various; Mary/Marie/Maria and Therese/Theresa/Teresa)

Mayca (Spanish; Maria + Carmen)

Milou (Dutch, French; Marie + Louise)

Mylène (French; Marie-Hélène)

And some non-Mary mashup Marian names I've seen include:

Dorolinda (Spanish; Dorotea + Linda)

Fiatalinda (Spanish; Fiat + Linda)

Index of names
Girls

Index of names
Boys

Bibliography

"About Edel." https://www.edelgathering.com/edel-gathering-details (accessed April 19, 2017).

Agreda, Venerable Mary of. *The Mystical City of God.* Charlotte, NC: TAN Books and Publishers, 2008.

Arthur, Adelaide. "Africa's Naming Traditions: Nine Ways To Name Your Child." BBC News, December 30, 2016. http://www.bbc.com/news/world-africa-37912748 (accessed April 19, 2017).

"The Angelus." Marians of the Immaculate Conception. http://www.marian.org/mary/prayers/angelus.php (accessed April 19, 2017).

Appellation Mountain. http://appellationmountain.net.

"Ave Maris Stella." http://www.ewtn.com/library/PRAYER/STAR.TXT (accessed April 19, 2017).

Baby Names of Ireland. http://www.babynamesofireland.com.

Baby Name Wizard. http://www.babynamewizard.com.

Basilika Mariazell. http://www.basilika-mariazell.at.

Behind the Name — The Etymology and History of First Names. http://www.behindthename.com.

Bergström-Allen, Johan, ed. *Climbing the Mountain: The Carmelite Journey.* St. Albert's Press, 2010. http://www.carmelite.org/documents/Spirituality/ctm06elijah.pdf (accessed April 19, 2017).

Bonaventure, St. "Mirror of the Blessed Virgin Mary." https://www.ewtn.com/library/SOURCES/MIRROR.TXT (accessed April 19, 2017).

"A Brief History." Catholic National Shrine of Our Lady — The Basilica of Our Lady, Walsingham. http://www.walsingham.org.uk/a-brief-history (accessed October 14, 2017).

Brownian, Carrie-Anne. "A Primer on Jèrriais Names." https://carrieannebrownian.wordpress.com/2017/02/17/a-primer-on-jerriais-names (accessed April 19, 2017).

Calloway, Donald H., MIC. *Champions of the Rosary: The History and Heroes of a Spiritual Weapon.* Stockbridge, MA: Marian Press, 2016.

"Casillas: Iker Casillas Fernández." Real Madrid. http://www.realmadrid.com/en/about-real-madrid/history/football-legends/iker-casillas-fernandez (accessed October 14, 2017).

The Catholic Encyclopedia. New York: Robert Appleton Company, 1907-1912. http://www.newadvent.org.

CatholicSaints.Info. http://catholicsaints.info.

Catholic Tradition. http://www.catholictradition.org.

Cecilia, Blessed. "The Miracles of St. Dominic." The Dominican Friars of the Province of St. Albert the Great. http://opcentral.org/blog/the-miracles-of-st-dominic (accessed April 24, 2017).

"The Chaplet of the Seven Sorrows." Marians of the Immaculate Conception. http://www.marian.org/mary/prayers/sorrows.php (accessed April 19, 2017).

Chrysostom, John. "An Address on Vainglory and the Right Way for Parents to Bring Up Their Children." Translated by M.L.W. Laistner. In *Christianity and Pagan Culture in the Later Roman Empire,* by M.L.W. Laistner. Ithaca: Cornell University Press, 1951.

Code of Canon Law. http://www.vatican.va/archive/ENG1104/_INDEX.HTM.

DePuy, W.H., ed. *Americanized Encylopaedia Britannica*. Vol. VII. Belford-Clarke Co., 1893, Chicago. Ebook, downloaded from Google Books April 18, 2017.

Greek Names. http://www.greek-names.info.

Dictionary by Merriam-Webster. https://www.merriam-webster.com.

DiProperzio, Linda. "What Your Child's Name Says About You." Parents (2011). http://www.parents.com/baby-names/ideas/getting-started/what-your-childs-name-says-about-you (accessed April 19, 2017).

Dodds, Monica and Bill. *Encyclopedia of Mary*. Huntington, IN: Our Sunday Visitor, 2007.

Edwards, George Wharton. *Vanished Halls and Cathedrals of France*. Philadelphia, PA: The Penn Publishing Co., 1917. Released as an eBook by Project Gutenberg in 2014. http://www.gutenberg.org/files/46069/46069-h/46069-h.htm (accessed April 19, 2017).

Emmons, Dennis. "What Is the Angelus?" *The Catholic Answer,* vol. 25, no. 2 (May/June 2011).hhttps://www.osv.com/RSS/365DaysToMercy/TabId/2752/ArtMID/21013/ArticleID/10353/What-Is-the-Angelus.aspx (accessed April 19, 2017).

Erlenbush, Father Ryan. "What Does the Name 'Mary' Mean?" The New Theological Movement (September 12, 2001). http://newtheologicalmovement.blogspot.com/2011/09/what-does-name-mary-mean.html (accessed October 29, 2017).

EWTN: Global Catholic Network. http://www.ewtn.com/.

Fagnant-MacArthur, Patrice. "The Feast of the Immaculate Heart of Mary." Catholic Mom (2013). http://catholicmom.com/2013/06/08/the-feast-of-the-immaculate-heart-of-mary (accessed April 19, 2017).

Fitzhenry, James. *Saint Fernando III: A Kingdom for Christ*. St. Mary's, KS: Catholic Vitality Publications, 2011.

Forvo: The Pronunciation Dictionary. https://forvo.com/.

"Greek Name Day Calendar." Greek Boston. http://www.greekboston.com/name-days/ (accessed April 19, 2017).

"Guide to Pronunciation." Merriam Webster. https://assets2.merriam-webster.com/mw/static/pdf/help/guide-to-pronunciation.pdf.

Hanks, Patrick, Kate Hardcastle, and Flavia Hodges, eds. *A Dictionary of First Names.* Oxford: Oxford University Press, 2006.

"Historical Summary." *Sanctuaire Notre-Dame-du-Cap.* https://www.sanctuaire-ndc.ca/en/nature-and-history/historical-summary (accessed October 14, 2017).

HowToPronounce. https://www.howtopronounce.com.

"International Workshop on the Scientific Approach to the Acheiropoietos Images." ENEA Research Center of Frascati (Italy) (May 4-6, 2010). http://www.acheiropoietos.info (accessed April 19, 2017).

"Irish Baby Names." Ireland Fun Facts! http://www.ireland-fun-facts.com/irish-baby-names.html (accessed April 19, 2017).

"Irish Surname – Murray." Ireland Roots. http://irelandroots.com/murray.htm (accessed April 19, 2017).

Knock Shrine. https://www.knockshrine.ie.

Koenig-Bricker, Woodeene. *A Saint's Name: A Comprehensive Listing of Christian and Biblical Names.* Skokie, IL: ACTA Publications, 2000.

Krymow, Vincenzina. *Mary's Flowers: Gardens, Legends & Meditations.* Phoenix, AZ: Amor Deus Publishing, 2010.

John Paul II, Pope St. "Apostolic Letter *Rosarium Virginis Mariae* of the Supreme Pontiff John Paul II to the Bishops, Clergy and Faithful on the Most Holy Rosary" (October 16, 2002). http://w2.vatican.va/content/john-paul-ii/en/apost_letters/2002/documents/hf_jp-ii_apl_20021016_rosarium-virginis-mariae.html (accessed April 19, 2017).

Lajoie, Ron. "Rose Hawthorne's Cause for Sainthood Moves to Rome." Catholic New York (April 17, 2013). http://cny.org/stories/Rose-Hawthornes-Cause-For-Sainthood-Moves-to-Rome,9204 (accessed April 19, 2017).

"Last Name: Gilmore." SurnameDB: The Internet Surname Database. http://www.surnamedb.com/Surname/Gilmore (accessed April 19, 2017).

"Latin Prayers." EWTN: Global Catholic Network. http://www.ewtn.com/library/prayer/latrosar.htm.

Liguori, St. Alphonsus. *The Glories of Mary.* New York: P.J. Kenedy & Sons, 1888. http://www.themostholyrosary.com/the-glories-of-mary.pdf (accessed April 19, 2017).

"List of Italian Female Given Names." Department of History and the Center for Family History & Genealogy (Brigham Young University). https://script.byu.edu/Documents/Nomi-Femminili.pdf (accessed April 18, 2017).

L'Italo-Americano. http://italoamericano.org/.

"The Little Office of the Blessed Virgin Mary." http://www.liturgies.net/Liturgies/Catholic/LittleOffice1.htm (accessed April 19, 2017).

The Liturgy of the Hours. New York: Catholic Book Publishing Corp., 1975.

"The Loreto Litanies." http://www.vatican.va/special/rosary/documents/litanie-lauretane_en.html.

"Lovely Lady Dressed in Blue." Catholic Tradition. http://www.catholictradition.org/Mary/lady-card.htm (accessed April 19, 2017).

Madre di Dio Incoronata: Basilica Sanctuario Madre di Dio Incoronata – Foggia. http://www.santuarioincoronata.it.

"Magnificat of Mary." Marians of the Immaculate Conception. http://www.marian.org/mary/prayers/canticle.php (accessed April 19, 2017).

Makwabe, Buyekezwa. "Pastor Dad's Prayers for Sexy Model." *SundayTimes* (June 10, 2012). http://www.pressreader.com/south-africa/sunday-times/20120610/281556582893037 (accessed April 19, 2017).

McLeod, the Rev. Xavier Donald. *History of the Devotion to the Blessed Virgin Mary in North America.* New York: Virtue & Yorston, 1866.

MeilleursPrénoms.com. http://meilleursprenoms.com.

Nameberry. https://nameberry.com.

The New American Bible, Revised Edition (NABRE). http://www.usccb.org/bible.

Nouvelle Évangélisation. http://nouvl.evangelisation.free.fr.

O'Growney, Eugene. "The 'Muls' and 'Gils': Some Irish Surnames," part II. *The Irish Ecclesiastical Record,* vol. III (1898). http://www.libraryireland.com/articles/Muls/MulsII.php (accessed April 19, 2017).

"Our Mother of Perpetual Help." The Redemptorists of the Baltimore Province. https://redemptorists.net/redemptorists/devotion-to-omph (accessed December 6, 2017).

Pius XII, Pope. "*Ad Caeli Reginam*: Encyclical of Pope Pius XII on Proclaiming the Queenship of Mary" (October 11, 1954).

"Popular Baby Names." Social Security Administration. https://www.ssa.gov/oact/babynames.

Pronouncekiwi. http://www.pronouncekiwi.com.

Pronounce Names. http://www.pronouncenames.com.

Reaney, P.H. and R.M Wilson. *A Dictionary of English Surnames.* Rev. 3rd Ed. Oxford: Oxford University Press, 1997.

Rengers, Christopher, O.F.M. Cap. with Dr. Matthew E. Bunson, K.H.S. *The 35 Doctors of the Church, Revised Edition.* Charlotte, NC: TAN Books, 2014. (E-book.)

Roman Catholic Saints. http://www.roman-catholic-saints.com.

Rosenkrantz, Linda, and Pamela Redmond Satran. *Beyond Shannon and Sean: An Enlightened Guide to Irish Baby Naming.* New York: St. Martin's Press, 1992.

Ryan, Joal. *Puffy, Xena, Quentin, Uma: And 10,000 Other Names for Your New Millennium Baby.* New York, NY: Plume, 1999.

"Salve Regina: English and Latin." EWTN: Global Catholic Network. https://www.ewtn.com/faith/teachings/maryd6d.htm (accessed April 19, 2017).

Sancta Nomina: Thoughts on Catholic Baby Naming. http://sanctanomina.net.

Santi, beati e testimoni. http://santiebeati.it.

Santoro, Nicholas J. *Mary in Our Life: Atlas of the Names and Titles of Mary, the*

Mother of Jesus, and Their Place in Marian Devotion. Bloomington, IN: iUniverse, Inc., 2011.

Schneider, Nathan. "The Angelus at Work." America (March 24, 2015). https://www.americamagazine.org/content/all-things/angelus-work (accessed December 29, 2017).

Sheehan, Rev. Thomas W. *Dictionary of Patron Saints' Names.* Huntington, IN: Our Sunday Visitor, 2001.

Towne, Katherine Morna. "Students' Painting Heads to Washington, D.C." *Saratoga TODAY,* (September 16, 2016), p. 21. https://issuu.com/saratogapublishing/docs/st091616-web/21 (accessed April 23, 2017).

University of Dayton: International Marian Research Institute. https://www.udayton.edu/imri.

Uckelman, S.L., ed. *The Dictionary of Medieval Names from European Sources.* http://dmnes.org.

"Venerable Edel Quinn." Presentata Curia of the Legion of Mary. http://legionofmaryd7.com/edelquinn.htm (accessed April 19, 2017).

Viquipèdia: L'enciclopèdia lliure. (Catalan) http://ca.wikipedia.org.

Wattenberg, Laura. *The Baby Name Wizard: A Magical Method for Finding the Perfect Name for Your Baby,* rev. 3rd ed. New York: Harmony Books, 2013.

Wattenberg, Laura. "The Surprising Story Behind One of the World's Top Brand Names." Baby Name Wizard (September 4, 2014). http://www.babynamewizard.com/archives/2014/9/the-surprising-story-behind-one-of-the-worlds-top-brand-names (accessed April 19, 2017).

Wikipedia: La encyclopedia libre. (Spanish) http://es.wikipedia.org.

Wikipedia: L'enciclopedia libera. (Italian) http://it.wikipedia.org.

Wikipédia: L'encyclopédie libre. (French) http://fr.wikipedia.org.

Wikipedia: The free encyclopedia. (English) http://en.wikipedia.org.

Withycombe, E.G. *The Oxford Dictionary of English Christian Names,* 3rd ed. Oxford: Oxford University Press, 1977.

Endnotes

1   Available at https://assets2.merriam-webster.com/mw/static/pdf/help/guide-to-pronunciation.pdf; http://www.behindthename.com; and http://forvo.com; see bibliography for other pronunciation sites.

2   Vincenzina Krymow, *Mary's Flowers: Gardens, Legends & Meditations*, (Phoenix, AZ: Amor Deus Publishing, 2010), p. 12. Used with permission.

3   Woodeene Koenig-Bricker, *A Saint's Name: A Comprehensive Listing of Christian and Biblical Names* (Skokie, IL: ACTA Publications, 2000), p. 6. Used with permission.

4   John Chrysostom, "An Address on Vainglory and the Right Way for Parents to Bring Up Their Children," trans. M.L.W. Laistner, in *Christianity and Pagan Culture in the Later Roman Empire*, by M.L.W. Laistner (Ithaca, NY: Cornell University Press, 1951), p. 108. Used with permission.

5   Fr. Calloway provides the source for King Jan's quote, "I came, I saw, God conquered!" as Robert Debs Heinl, Jr., *Dictionary of Military and Naval Quotations* (Annapolis, MD: United States Naval Institute, 1996), p. 65.

6   Donald H. Calloway, MIC, *Champions of the Rosary: The History and Heroes of a Spiritual Weapon* (Stockbridge, MA: Marian Press, 2016), pp. 98-99.

7   Frederick Holweck, "Feast of the Holy Name of Mary," *The Catholic Encyclopedia*, vol. 10. (New York: Robert Appleton Company, 1911), http://www.newadvent.org/cathen/10673b.htm.

8   "Popular Baby Names," Social Security Administration, https://www.ssa.gov/oact/babynames.

9   Hugh Henry, "Alma Redemptoris Mater," *The Catholic Encyclopedia*, vol. 1. (1907), http://www.newadvent.org/cathen/01326d.htm; Thomas W. Sheehan, Dictionary of Patron Saints' Names (Huntington, IN: Our Sunday Visitor, 2001), p. 26.

10   Calloway, p. 127.

11   Venerable Mary of Agreda, *The Mystical City of God* (Charlotte, NC: TAN Books and Publishers, 2008), p. 225.

12   St. Bonaventure, "Mirror of the Blessed Virgin Mary," https://www.ewtn.com/library/SOURCES/MIRROR.TXT; "The Little Office of the Blessed Virgin Mary," http://www.liturgies.net/Liturgies/Catholic/LittleOffice1.htm.

13   "Ave Maris Stella," http://www.ewtn.com/library/PRAYER/STAR.TXT.

14   Buyekezwa Makwabe, "Pastor Dad's Prayers for Sexy Model," *Sunday Times* (June 10, 2012), http://www.pressreader.com/south-africa/sunday-times/20120610/281556582893037.

15   Definition of *beatrix* from J. Uckelman, S.L. Uckelman, "Beatrice," in S.L. Uckelman, ed., *The Dictionary of Medieval Names from European Sources*, Edition 2017, no. 1. http://dmnes.org/2017/1/name/Beatrice. Additionally, I wanted to be sure it wasn't theologically inaccurate to say that Mary can be described as "she who blesses," so I found several instances in which St. John Paul II used that wording in his homilies: e.g., "Apostolic Pilgrimage to Nigeria, Benin Gabon and Equatorial Guinea: Mass for the Families: Homily of John Paul II" (February 13, 1982), https://w2.vatican.va/content/john-paul-ii/en/homilies/1982/documents/hf_jp-ii_hom_19820213_onitsha-nigeria.html; "Apostolic Journey to the Philippines, Papua New Guinea, Australia and Sri Lanka: Liturgy of the Word for the Sick and the Suffering: Homily of the Holy Father John Paul II" (January 18, 1996), https://w2.vatican.va/content/john-paul-ii/en/homilies/1995/documents/hf_jp-ii_hom_19950118_boroko.html; "Viaje Apostólico a México y Curaçao: Santa Misa para los Jóvenes en la Explanada de << El

Rosario>>: Homilía del Santo Padre Juan Pablo II" (May 8, 1990), https://w2.vatican.va/content/john-paul-ii/es/homilies/1990/documents/hf_jp-ii_hom_19900508_san-juan-de-los-lagos.html (all accessed October 12, 2017).

[16] Frederick Holweck, "Immaculate Conception," *The Catholic Encyclopedia*, vol. 7. (1910), http://www.newadvent.org/cathen/07674d.htm.

[17] "Despoina," Greek Names, http://www.greek-names.info/despoina.

[18] Calloway, p. 89.

[19] "Venerable Edel Quinn," Presentata Curia of the Legion of Mary, http://legionofmaryd7.com/edelquinn.htm.

[20] "About Edel," https://www.edelgathering.com/edel-gathering-details.

[21] Cf. *Jn* 1:12-18; 17:3; *Rom* 8:14-17; 2 Pet 1:3-4.

[22] Adelaide Arthur, "Africa's Naming Traditions: Nine Ways to Name Your Child," BBC News (December 30, 2016), http://www.bbc.com/news/world-africa-37912748.

[23] Monica & Bill Dodds, *Encyclopedia of Mary* (Huntington, IN: Our Sunday Visitor, 2007), p. 226.

[24] "Celebrity Guest: Hope from *Hope and Justin*," *Sancta Nomina* (November 1, 2016), https://sanctanomina.net/2016/11/01/celebrity-guest-hope-from-hope-and-justin/; see also http://www.hopeandjustin.com.

[25] "Maebh," Baby Names of Ireland, http://www.babynamesofireland.com/maebh.

[26] John S. Johnson, *The Rosary in Action* (Charlotte, NC: TAN Books and Publishers, 1977), p. 26, as quoted in Calloway, p. 176.

[27] "Baby Name Consultant: Mary, Music, and Ends-in-a," *Sancta Nomina* (November 10, 2016), https://sanctanomina.net/2016/10/17/baby-name-consultant-mary-music-and-ends-in-a/comment-page-1/#comment-11499.

[28] "Mary," Behind the Name, http://www.behindthename.com/name/mary; Anthony Maas, "The Name of Mary," *The Catholic Encyclopedia*, vol. 15, (1912), http://www.newadvent.org/cathen/15464a.htm.

[29] St. Alphonsus Liguori, *The Glories of Mary* (New York: P.J. Kenedy & Sons, 1888), pp. 320-321

[30] Laura Wattenberg, "The Surprising Story Behind One of the World's Top Brand Names," *Baby Name Wizard* (September 4, 2014), http://www.babynamewizard.com/archives/2014/9/the-surprising-story-behind-one-of-the-worlds-top-brand-names.

[31] Father Ryan Erlenbush, "What Does the Name 'Mary' Mean?" The New Theological Movement (September 12, 2001), http://newtheologicalmovement.blogspot.com/2011/09/what-does-name-mary-mean.html.

[32] *LG* 56.

[33] Katherine Morna Towne, "Students' Painting Heads to Washington, D.C.," *Saratoga TODAY* (September 16, 2016), p. 21, https://issuu.com/saratogapublishing/docs/st091616-web/21.

[34] Calloway, p. 400, footnote no. 35.

[35] James Fitzhenry, *Saint Fernando III: A Kingdom for Christ* (St. Mary's, KS: Catholic Vitality Publications, 2011), pp. 308–313, 319, 339.

[36] "Wee Lassie's Debut!" *Sancta Nomina* (March 24, 2015), https://sanctanomina.net/2015/03/24/wee-lassies-debut/.

[37] Information shared in a comment left on this discussion board: http://www.babynamewizard.com/forum/what-do-you-think-of-these-names-slightly-unusual. The information was verified by an online search — I found several obituaries for women named Rosary from Louisiana.

[38] Francis Gigot, "Seraphim," *The Catholic Encyclopedia*, vol. 13 (1912), http://www.newadvent.org/cathen/13725b.htm.

[39] Towne, p. 21.

[40] Calloway, p. 44.

[41] W.H. DePuy, ed., *Americanized Encylopaedia Britannica*, vol. VII (Chicago: Bel ford-Clarke Co., 1893), p. 3906, https://books.google.com/books?id = A_hMAQAAMAA J&pg = PA3906&lpg = PA3906&dq = notre + dame + de + la + trielle&source = bl&ots = o9gVoopU7R&sig = eUuT6czWrbFJQ360u1q3urUBM_k&hl = en&sa = X&ved = 0ahUKEwib7Jf97JXTAhVFSiYKHQ5oA1kQ6AEIOjAJ#v = onepage&q = notre%20dame%20 de%20la%20trielle&f=false; George Wharton Edwards, Vanished Halls and Cathedrals of France, originally published 1917 (Philadelphia, PA: The Penn Publishing Co.), released as an eBook by Project Gutenberg in 2014, http://www.gutenberg.org/files/46069/46069-h/46069-h.htm; Bartholomew Randolph, "Philibert Vrau," *The Catholic Encyclopedia*, vol. 15. (1912), http://www.newadvent.org/cathen/15514a.htm.

[42] "Celebrity Guest: Katheryn, Expert on Naming and Adoption," *Sancta Nomina* (September 20, 2016), https://sanctanomina.net/2016/09/20/celebrity-guest-katheryn-expert-on-naming-and-adoption.

[43] Krymow, p. 113. Used with permission.

[44] Cf. DS 291; 294; 427; 442; 503; 571; 1880.

[45] *LG* 57.

[46] Cf. *LG* 52.

[47] Cf. *Mk* 3:31-35; 6:3; 1 *Cor* 9:5; *Gal* 1:19.

[48] *Mt* 13:55; 28:1; cf. *Mt* 27:56.

[49] Cf. *Gen* 13:8; 14:16; 29:15; etc.

[50] Calloway, p. 199.

[51] Ibid., pp. 112, 214.

[52] Dennis Emmons, "What Is the Angelus?" The Catholic Answer, vol. 25, no. 2 (May/June 2011), https://www.osv.com/RSS/365DaysToMercy/TabId/2752/ArtMID/21013/ArticleID/10353/What-Is-the-Angelus.aspx. Used with permission.

[53] Nathan Schneider, "The Angelus at Work," *America* (March 24, 2015), https://www.americamagazine.org/content/all-things/angelus-work.

[54] Christopher Rengers, O.F.M. Cap. with Dr. Matthew E. Bunson, K.H.S., *The 35 Doctors of the Church, Revised Edition*, (Charlotte, NC: TAN Books, 2014), p. 364. (E-book.)

[55] "March CatholicMom Article up Today!" *Sancta Nomina* (March 15, 2017), https://sanctanomina.net/2017/03/15/march-catholicmom-article-up-today-%E2%98%98/#comment-13525.

[56] Calloway, pp. 130-131.

[57] John Paul II, "Apostolic Letter *Rosarium Virginis Mariae* of the Supreme Pontiff John Paul II to the Bishops, Clergy and Faithful on the Most Holy Rosary" (October 16, 2002), http://w2.vatican.va/content/john-paul-ii/en/apost_letters/2002/documents/hf_jp-ii_apl_20021016_rosarium-virginis-mariae.html.

[58] Calloway, p. 325.

[59] Ibid., p. 156.

[60] "Historical Summary," *Sanctuaire Notre-Dame-du-Cap*, https://www.sanctuaire-ndc.ca/en/nature-and-history/historical-summary.

[61] Calloway, p. 192.

[62] E.G. Withycombe, *The Oxford Dictionary of English Christian Names*, 3rd ed. (Oxford: Oxford University Press, 1977), p. 90.

[63] Liguori, p. 63.

[64] Johan Bergström-Allen, ed., *Climbing the Mountain: The Carmelite Journey*, (Faversham, Kent, UK: St. Albert's Press, 2010), p. 122. http://www.carmelite.org/documents/Spirituality/ctm06elijah.pdf.

[65] Calloway, p. 259.

[66] Ibid., p. 308.

[67] "Casillas: Iker Casillas Fernández," *Real Madrid*, http://www.realmadrid.com/en/about-real-madrid/history/football-legends/iker-casillas-fernandez.

[68] Calloway, p. 169.

[69] Ibid., pp. 251-252.

[70] Ibid., p. 229.

[71] Ibid., p. 208.

[72] Blessed Cecilia, "The Miracles of St. Dominic," the Dominican Friars of the Province of St. Albert the Great, http://opcentral.org/blog/the-miracles-of-st-dominic.

[73] Hanks, Hardcastle, and Hodges, *A Dictionary of First Names* (Oxford: Oxford University Press, 2006), p. 193.

[74] Ibid., p. 381.

[75] "Nunzio," Behind the Name, http://www.behindthename.com/name/nunzio.

[76] Calloway, pp. 157, 298.

[77] Ibid., p. 298.

[78] Ibid., p. 204.

[79] Ibid., p. 206.

[80] Hanks, Hardcastle, and Hodges, p. 228.

[81] Calloway, pp. 162-163.

[82] Fitzhenry, pp. 308-313, 319, 339.

[83] Gigot, "Seraphim."

[84] Joseph Hilgers, "Scapular," *The Catholic Encyclopedia*, vol. 13. Robert Appleton Company, 1912, New York, http://www.newadvent.org/cathen/13508b.htm.

[85] Dodds, p. 295.

[86] "A Brief History," Catholic National Shrine of Our Lady — The Basilica of Our Lady, Walsingham, http://www.walsingham.org.uk/a-brief-history.

Acknowledgments and Thanks

I have so many people to thank for their help in the writing of this book!

My parents' first priority was to bring their children up in the faith; they have also always encouraged us to cultivate and share the gifts and strengths that God has given us. All that I have first began with their decisions as spouses and parents, and so much of my life's path has been determined through their help and encouragement, so my very first thanks goes to them. A girl couldn't ask for a better Mom and Dad, nor for a better Nannie and Poppie for her children.

My sweet friend Joanna ignited the spark that became this book when she told me her oldest daughter's name: Faith Immaculata. Joanna opened up a whole world of possibilities with that one bit of information, and I started researching and compiling Marian names almost immediately. That was nearly 10 years ago!

This book wouldn't have been possible without the success of my blog, *Sancta Nomina: Thoughts on Catholic baby naming* (SanctaNomina.net), which was due entirely to the grace of God — I certainly couldn't have made it happen. He allowed the following people to play key roles, for which I'm so grateful:

- **Kira**, one of my closest friends and the first regular reader of my blog (besides my mom). Her suggestions and support, from the very beginning through to the present, have been invaluable.
- **Abby Sandel**, founder of Appellation Mountain (AppellationMountain.net) and columnist at Nameberry.com, who has been one of my biggest cheerleaders, as she is for all of us who have name blogs/sites — like a loving mother, she encourages us and shares our successes with her own readers. Abby introduced me to **Linda Rosenkrantz**, co-founder of Nameberry, and helped brainstorm some ideas I could write about for that eminent name site. Since then, I've had many conversations with Linda over email regarding pieces I've written for Nameberry. Like Abby, she's always been responsive and encouraging, despite the fact that I'm a fairly new player in the name world and she's been leading the field for twenty years. **Laura Wattenberg**, author of *The Baby Name Wizard* (book and web site), and **Dr. Sara Uckelman**, editor-in-chief of the *Dictionary of Medieval Names from European Sources* (dmnes.org), both of whose research and insights have greatly helped my own. **Lisa Hendey** at CatholicMom.com, who accepted me as a monthly columnist writing about Catholic names when my blog was new, and **Barb Szyszkiewicz**, my editor at CatholicMom.com, who has been incredibly helpful — a wonderful mentor as a Catholic writer. So many in the online Catholic world and social media who have given invaluable help to me both in the growth

of my blog and in the promotion of this book, and several who were inspiring to me in writing, motherhood, and faith long before I ever even had a blog! This list is in alphabetical order by last name, not by importance: **Rachel Balducci, Danielle Bean, Lindsay Boever, Dwija Borobia, Sharon Clark, Micaela Darr, Simcha Fisher** (for whom I did my very first baby name consultation, and when she shared it with her readers, I suddenly had readers! It's all snowballed from there), **Jennifer Fulwiler, Christy Isinger, Colleen Martin, Heather McQuillan, Grace Patton, Mandi Richards, Haley Stewart, Tommy Tighe, Jenny Uebbing, JoAnna Wahlund, and Kate Wicker.**

And of course, some of the most important people involved in this process are my dear readers. To all of you: I love your excitement and enthusiasm, and your ideas! You all have so many ideas that I'd never thought of before! Whether they're just names you've scribbled down on your own list for daydreams and/or the future, or names you've actually given your children, I've been inspired, and inspired, and inspired again by your creativity and faith. I've loved helping you name your babies, I've loved hearing your name stories, I've loved working through your questions and concerns with you, and I've loved seeing your brilliance in the comments on my posts. I've learned from you, my faith has been strengthened by you, and this book is a hundred times better than it would have been without you. Thank you, thank you! I could never name all of you — I'd dread missing someone — but I do just have to mention those whose experiences and/or ideas were specifically mentioned in this book: Mrs. S. (Rosey's mom), Lindsay B., Grace S., Mary M., Katheryn C., Joanna S., Amy E., Catherine P., Hope S., Jen G., Amy O., Laura T., Clare B., Theresa H., Emily G., Lauren W., Erika X., Theresa C., Amy and Heidi (whose last names I don't know), and one whose name is unknown (handle: testhair). I have a few friends who aren't readers of the blog who also contributed their name stories: Phonsey L. and Ginny B. And I offer a special thanks to all those who have emailed me over the past few years asking for posts on Marian names — it helped me and Marian Press to know that this book would indeed fill a hole in the name-book market, as well as be a nice addition to the genre of Marian books.

To Marian Press: Thank you for taking a chance on me! I'm particularly grateful to those with whom I've had personal interactions: Chris Sparks, who originally saw promise in my proposed project; Joan Lamar, who helped me through many months of extensive revisions and additions; Tad Floridis, who has patiently explained the business/marketing side; and Mary Clark, who has grabbed my hand and finished the race with me, helping me through all the nitty gritty final details. I hope I don't disappoint! I'm so honored and humbled to have my book associated with the Marian Fathers.

A very special and bittersweet thanks goes to my old college writing professor and post-college writing mentor, Naton Leslie, whose professional advice and willingness to field my emails for years and even meet up to talk shop (writ-

ing) over coffee was a treasure and a gift, and whose input I'd always hoped to continue receiving. I still pray for the repose of his soul, gone just about exactly four years as I type this, and I'm still working on the project he was helping me with — someday, by God's grace, I'll finish it!

I want to thank my wonderful bishop, Bishop Ed Scharfenberger, who was already nodding his head "yes" before I even finished asking him if he'd consider taking a look at the manuscript to see if he'd feel comfortable offering his endorsement. Our diocese is so blessed to have him at the helm.

Thank you to the patrons of my writing efforts — St. John Paul the Great, St. Gianna, and St. Francis de Sales — and to the patroness of my blog, St. Anne. I've relied heavily on their intercession to keep me focused, balanced, wise, and prudent.

Thank you to my siblings, who have each supported and encouraged me in their own ways: Ben, Jeb, Molly, Stevie, and Bess. Growing up with all of you made me want to have a big family of my own (and give my children similarly amazing names!). Stevie and Bess have been especially fun to talk names with — they love names like I do. Thank you to my sisters-in-law, Molly and Hailey, for jumping into name conversations with me whenever we're together, and also over text, and for letting me spotlight my nephews' and niece's names on the blog. Thank you to my brother-in-law, Mark, who has constantly and consistently shown real interest in the progress of my book — he never fails to ask how it's going. Thank you to Fr. James Ebert, my dear friend and my boys' honorary uncle, who has promised to promote this book to every expectant couple he encounters. Thank you to my oldest friend, Stephanie, whose prayers and support have helped me immeasurably throughout the process of writing this book. Thank you to my extended family and my wonderful friends, who have always been excited to hear of each new development in my writing endeavors.

I'd like to mention my maternal grandmother, Annie Oakley, who always wanted to be a writer, and who passed on her interest and talent to my mom, who is an Irish poet and lover of literary beauty — a good deal of whatever abilities I have as a writer surely came from them.

I must also mention how important my dad's creative thinking, professional advice, integrity, and the way he orders his priorities (we know he does all of it for us!) have been for me.

Finally, thank you to my husband for all those Saturdays and evenings when he masterfully held down the fort so I could work (I spent eight to 10 hours many a Saturday at the library!) — how else could I have finished this book? He is the definition of a supportive husband, and an incredible model for our boys. Thank you, too, to my boys, each of whom I love more than I can say; each of whom has been excited for me that I wrote a book; and each of whom has brought me closer to Heaven (and whose names gave me such great pleasure to help choose).

My soul proclaims the greatness of the Lord, my spirit exalts in God my Savior, for He has looked with favor on his lowly servant.